GLORY
GROW
GO

Life as a Disciple of Christ

Branden W. Ford

Glory Grow Go: Life as a Disciple of Christ

Copyright © 2021 by Branden W. Ford

April 10, 2021

Religion > Christian Life > Spiritual Growth
Religion > Christian Theology > General

ISBN: 978-0-578-89595-6

TABLE OF CONTENTS

Acknowledgments

This book is dedicated to our Glorious God. Without Him, I would have remained a wretched sinner lost in this world. It is only due to the saving atonement of Christ on the cross that I am able to enjoy a genuine relationship with God. It is out of the enjoyment of this restored relationship that I am even able to write this book. I write this book for God's glory, the credit of any wisdom and help that this book may bring to others belongs to God. To Him be all the glory. I simply served as a servant of God. This book is the product of what God taught me through Scripture, prayer, and the people that He placed in my life. I would like to give a special thank you to those people.

Thank you, Chaplain Joshua Chittim and Chaplain Jared Vineyard, for faithfully proclaiming the Gospel and for your continual mentorship, discipleship, and friendship. I suspect that many of the words and principles taught in this book will look familiar to you.

Thank you, Pastor Bubba Jennings, for your leadership. This book is in many ways the product of the discipleship I received during my time at Resurrection Church.

Thank you, Aaron & Ciera Madasz, for serving as my editing workgroup. I deeply appreciate your time and support. I am thankful for our friendship and for your willingness to sacrifice many of your Sunday afternoons to help me edit this book.

Thank you to those who read the early drafts of this book: Uncle David Ford, Chaplain Mark Levine, Chaplain Kevin Betton, Angela Casteel, James Bailey, Jeffery Terhune, and James Murray. Your feedback was invaluable and greatly appreciated.

Introduction
Discipleship and the Gospel

"For the love of Christ controls us, because we have concluded this: that one has died for all, therefore all have died; and He died for all, that those who live might no longer live for themselves but for Him who for their sake died and was raised."
~ 2 Corinthians 5:14-15

<u>DISCIPLESHIP</u>

What does it mean to be a Disciple of Christ?

A disciple is a follower and a student of a mentor. While the word disciple can simply mean student, I will use the word to mean more than just the average student/teacher relationship. Often, a disciple will dedicate their life to the goals and mission of their mentor and pass on what they have learned so that others may continue the mission. Discipleship is a life-long process where the disciple disciplines their body, mind, and soul to reflect the ways of their mentor's teachings. Therefore, to be a Disciple of Christ is to be a follower and student of Jesus, who is the Christ.[1] Disciples of Christ dedicate their lives to Christ and His mission. They will discipline their body, mind, and soul to reflect Christ and His way.

Before I go any further on this topic, I would like to take the time now to explore why anyone would embrace this discipleship. Why would anyone submit to a teacher who had been arrested and condemned to execution for his teachings two thousand years ago? Why would anyone follow and dedicate their lives to Jesus?

The answer to this question is found in the gospel.

---

[1] **Christ:** Anointed One. Messiah is the Hebrew word for "Anointed One."

7

THE GOSPEL

When Christians speak of the gospel, they are referring to the Good News that **Jesus came and died for the sins of mankind so that we may enjoy a genuine relationship with God. Then Jesus was resurrected on the third day of His death, proving that He was who He claimed to be, and that He accomplished what He set out to accomplish.**
I would encourage you to go back and reread that last paragraph, do not just skim over it. Yes, the term and concept may be familiar, but it is of great significance. [2]

Now that you have reread the definition of the gospel, let's unpack it to provide a little more explanation.

Jesus came: I began by stating that Jesus came... but came from where? To understand where Jesus came from, we first need to understand that Jesus is God! Scripture reveals that God is a Triune being, meaning that while there is only one God, He eternally exists as three distinct persons: Father, Son, and Holy Spirit. Each person of the Trinity is distinct from the other, and each are fully God. Yet there is only one God. [3] Jesus is God the Son and He existed before all creation. In fact, all things were created by Jesus.[4]
Jesus then became a man and came to earth. The Gospel of John puts it this way, "In the beginning was the Word, and the Word was with God, and the Word was God... And the Word became flesh and dwelt among us, and we have seen

---

[2] The word "gospel" is of Greek origins which simply means, "good news." Admittedly, Christians can be guilty of overusing this word in such a general sense that it almost dilutes the word's actual meaning. The gospel is the specific message that Jesus came and died for our sins to bring us into relationship with Him.

[3] **Trinity:** "God eternally exists as three persons, Father, Son, and Holy Spirit, and each person is fully God, and there is one God" (Grudem, *Systematic Theology*, 269).

[4] John 1:3 states, "All things were made through Him, and without Him was not anything made that was made." Cross reference with Colossians 1:16-17.

His glory, glory as of the only Son from the Father, full of grace and truth."[5] God took on flesh and became a man. In becoming a man, Jesus did not lose His divine nature; rather, He gained a human nature. Thus, Jesus is fully God and fully man.[6] Therefore, Jesus is God who came from His heavenly throne and came to earth by becoming a man.

And died for the sins of mankind: To understand why Jesus left His throne and became man, we need to understand the situation of mankind.

The first chapter of Genesis describes how God created all things and after He created all things, He declared that it was all "very good."[7] Yet, all we have to do is look around and we can tell that creation is no longer "very good." So... what happened?

Sin happened.[8] The first created people, Adam and Eve, disobeyed God by eating fruit that they were explicitly commanded not to eat.[9] This act brought sin into the world and contaminated all of mankind and all creation with sin. Since the time of Adam and Eve, all people have been born with a sinful nature, a nature that desires to defy God.[10] Due to this inherent sinful nature, Scripture teaches us that "all have sinned and fall short of the glory of God."[11] We do not

---

[5] John 1:1, 14.

[6] Theologians refer to the two natures of Christ as the hypostatic union.
Hypostatic Union: "The union of Christ's human and divine natures in one person" (Grudem, *Systematic Theology*, 695).

[7] Genesis 1:31 states, "And God saw everything that He had made, and behold, it was very good. And there was evening and there was morning, the sixth day."

[8] **Sin:** Miss the mark; fall short of God's glory. To rebel against God. "Any failure to conform to the moral law of God in act, attitude, or nature" (Grudem, *Systematic Theology*, 619).

[9] Genesis 3:6 states, "So when the woman saw that the tree was good for food, and that it was a delight to the eyes, and that the tree was to be desired to make one wise, she took of its fruit and ate, and she also gave some to her husband who was with her, and he ate."

[10] Romans 5:18-19 states that "one trespass led to condemnation for all men" and "by the one man's disobedience the many were made sinners."

[11] Romans 3:23.

measure up to God's perfect righteousness, none of us have lived a perfect life, nor are we able to. We are infected with sin. This infection is rooted in our heart. In our fallen state our very identity has been contaminated. As R.C. Sproul once said, "We are not sinners because we sin. We sin because we are sinners.[12]

Since we have all sinned, we should all wonder: what is the consequence of sin? The prophet Isaiah answers this question stating, "your iniquities have made a separation between you and your God, and your sins have hidden His face from you so that He does not hear."[13] Due to sin, we are separated from God, the giver and sustainer of life. What do you suppose would happen to a creature that is separated from the One who sustains their life? It would die. Death is the product of our separation with God, since sin separates us from Him whom gives and sustains our life. As Scripture states, "the wages of sin is death."[14]

Furthermore, God is a God of justice. Sin is to rebel against God. It is treason against the Lord of all creation. Therefore, God's justice demands that sinners deserve to receive His wrath, "for the wrath of God is revealed from heaven against all ungodliness and unrighteousness of men, who by their unrighteousness suppress the truth."[15] Thus, hell is the place of eternal damnation for all who rebel against God.

If the consequence for sin is death, and all have sinned, then that means that all deserve death! That means I deserve death! That means you deserve death! What hope do we have? We have none in our own strength nor in our own merit. We cannot undo the sins that we have committed.

---

[12] R.C. Sproul, "We Are Not Sinners Because We Sin. We Sin Because We Are Sinners.," *Twitter* (Twitter, October 3, 2017), last modified October 3, 2017, accessed January 1, 2021,
https://twitter.com/rcsproul/status/915249707974365184?lang=en.
[13] Isaiah 59:2.
[14] Romans 6:23.
[15] Romans 1:18.

There is nothing that we can do to atone for our sins. Sin has taken root into our heart, causing each of us to be born with a sinful nature. Furthermore, there is nothing we can do to rid ourselves of our sinful nature. Our only hope is in the mercy and grace of God.[16]

The Good News is that God is not only a God of justice, but also a God of love. In His love, God offers us grace and decided to forgive us of our sins. However, since God is a God of justice, He could not just ignore our sins. Our sins demanded a payment... death. It is at the cross that the love of God and the justice of God come to a climax. Due to God's love for us, Jesus became a man with the purpose of being the perfect sacrifice for sin. Jesus lived a righteous life in perfect obedience to God's law. When Jesus died on the cross, He was not dying for His own sins since He was completely without sin. Therefore, Jesus' death was able to cover the sins of others.

The cross was not an accident, it was Jesus' mission. While it was man who condemned Jesus to death, it was Jesus' plan to lay down His life to save mankind. At the cross, Jesus shows us God's love by taking our sins upon Himself and dying the death that we deserved so that the justice of God would be satisfied. Paul explained this concept by writing, "and you, who were dead in your trespasses and the uncircumcision of your flesh, God made alive together with Him, having forgiven us all our trespasses, by canceling the record of debt that stood against us with its legal demands. This He set aside, nailing to the cross."[17]

So that we may enjoy a genuine relationship with God: Why did Jesus die on the cross? What did Jesus come to accomplish? Jesus explained His mission to a man named

---

[16] **Grace:** Undeserved and unearned love. "God's goodness toward those who deserve only punishment" (Grudem, *Systematic Theology*, 239).
[17] Colossians 2:13-14.

Nicodemus, where He states, "For God so loved the world, that He gave His only Son, that whoever believes in Him should not perish but have eternal life."[18] This verse may be familiar to you but think about what Jesus is stating. He is stating that because God the Father loved His creation, He sent Jesus (God the Son) to save us from our punishment. Jesus was sent to die on the cross in order to give eternal life to those who receive Christ through faith.

In our sin, we deserve death and hell. Yet, God is full of grace and sent Jesus to live the life that we should have lived and died that death that we deserved to give us eternal life. Scripture states that, "the wages of sin is death, but the free gift of God is eternal life in Christ Jesus our Lord."[19] We do not deserve eternal life, nor can we earn it. Through Christ, God offers salvation to mankind as a free gift. We receive this free gift through faith. Jesus even stated that only those who "believe in Him" will have eternal life. Scripture states, "since we have been justified by faith, we have peace with God through our Lord Jesus Christ. Through Him we have also obtained access by faith into this grace in which we stand, and we rejoice in hope of the glory of God."[20] It is only through faith in Christ that we can have peace with God and receive the eternal life that Christ offers us.

But what is eternal life? Is it to live forever? Is it to go to heaven? What did Jesus mean by this phrase?

Fortunately, we do not need to speculate what Jesus meant because near the end of His earthly ministry Jesus explained exactly what He meant by the phrase "eternal life." The night before Jesus was crucified, He prayed to God the Father on behalf of His disciples. Near the beginning of this prayer He defined eternal life by stating, "And this is eternal life, that they know You, the only true God, and Jesus

---

[18] John 3:16.
[19] Romans 6:23.
[20] Romans 5:1-2.

Christ whom You have sent."[21] Jesus defines eternal life as knowing God. Notice that it is not to "know *about* God," nor is it to "know *of* God," rather Jesus said eternal life is to "know You, the only true God." This is relational language. Jesus is saying that eternal life is about having a true genuine relationship with God!

If we really think about it, this should make perfect sense. It should follow that since the cross paid the penalty of sin, then we should be reunited with God and thus our relationship with God should be restored. If death is the consequence of our separation with God, then life should be the product of our restored relationship with God. Notice that the focus of eternal life is about having a genuine relationship with God (living forever with God is simply a byproduct of this relationship). This means that eternal life starts the moment we have faith in Christ's atonement![22] In that moment, we begin to enjoy our relationship with God. This means that if you have true faith in Christ, then your new life, shaped and influenced by this restored relationship, has already begun!

Then Jesus was resurrected on the third day of His death, proving that He was who He claimed to be, and that He accomplished what He set out to accomplish: Jesus' story does not end with His death. On the third day of His death, Jesus was resurrected, lived with His disciples for forty days after His resurrection, ascended back to heaven, and now sits on His throne at the right hand of God the Father.

It is in Jesus' death that the punishment of our sin is paid; therefore, it is in His death that we are saved. However, it is in His resurrection that we can have assurance of this salvation. The resurrection is the proof of purchase that our

---

[21] John 17:3; on a personal note, this is my favorite verse in the Bible.

[22] **Atonement:** Reconciliation. "The work Christ did in His life and death to earn our salvation" (Grudem, *Systematic Theology*, 705).

sins have been paid. Furthermore, the resurrection affirms that Jesus is in fact who He claims to be, which is God! Lastly, the resurrection testifies that all of Jesus' teachings, power, and the eternal life that He offers us are all true. We can place our hope and trust in Jesus as our Lord and Savior because He was resurrected.

BEING A DISCIPLE OF CHRIST

Those who submit to Christ and receive His salvation through faith are Disciples of Christ. Disciples of Christ submit and follow Jesus because Jesus is God. He created us, He continues to sustain us, He is perfect in all ways, He is the definer of truth, and loves us so much that He became a man to die for us. By His blood we are saved from our sins and our relationship with God is restored! The life of a Disciple of Christ should reflect this truth.

As a Disciple of Christ, we should embrace Jesus as our Lord and Savior by embracing our restored relationship with God. But what does this look like? What does it mean to be a Disciple of Christ? What is the purpose of being a Disciple of Christ? How does a Disciple of Christ reflect Christ? How does a Disciple of Christ carry out Jesus' mission? These questions bring us to the purpose of this book.

The purpose of being a Disciple of Christ is to give **glory** to Christ. We reflect Christ as we **grow** in relationship with Christ, which in turn causes us to grow to be more like Christ. Lastly, we carry out the mission of Christ when we **go** out to declare the gospel to the rest of the world that others may come to know and glorify God in a true genuine relationship. Therefore, being a Disciple of Christ can be summarized by using three key statements:

Glory to Christ
Grow in Christ
Go for Christ

PART I
GLORY TO CHRIST

"So, whether you eat or drink, or whatever you do, do all to
the **GLORY** of God."
~ 1 Corinthians 10:31

Chapter 1
Glory To Christ: The Foundational Purpose

GLORIFY GOD

When building a structure, the first thing that you do is lay out the foundation. Everything else is then built on that foundation. The foundation is the most essential part of any building since it must support the rest of the structure. Regardless of how beautiful a building may appear, if something is wrong with the foundation then the whole building will eventually fall apart. Therefore, as we begin our study on what it means to be a Disciple of Christ, we must start by carefully laying out the foundation.

The foundational purpose of being a Disciple of Christ is to give glory to God. Glorifying Christ must be our first and foremost concern. It should drive everything we do, think, and believe.

To glorify God means to praise, honor, and worship God. Scripture tells us to "ascribe to the LORD, O families of the peoples, ascribe to the LORD glory and strength! Ascribe to the LORD the glory due His name; bring an offering and come before Him! Worship the LORD in the splendor of holiness."[1] This passage provides three key elements in how we are to glorify God.

First, it repeatedly states to "ascribe to the LORD glory," which means to recognize God as the most important being who deserves all our praise and is to be given the highest honor. We are to give Him credit for all His greatness and to acknowledge God as the source of all the many blessings that He provides us.

The passage goes on to explain that we glorify God when we "bring an offering" to Him. This offering usually referred to an animal sacrifice for the atonement of sins (among other

---

[1] 1 Chronicles 16:28-29.

reasons).[2] However, Jesus' sacrificial offering of Himself on the cross was so great that it perfectly appeased the justice of God for our sins and fulfilled this requirement. Scripture states that "we have been sanctified through the offering of the body of Jesus Christ once for all... for by a single offering He has perfected for all time those who are being sanctified."[3] Jesus offered Himself as the perfect sacrifice on the cross.

While we no longer need to bring an animal sacrifice as an offering to God, we can still "bring an offering" to God. Scripture explains that "through Him then let us continually offer up a sacrifice of praise to God, that is, the fruit of lips that acknowledge His name. Do not neglect to do good and to share what you have, for such sacrifices are pleasing to God."[4] The heart of the offering is about glorifying God through praise, submission, and faithfulness, recognizing that He is God and that we are His creation.

Lastly, the verse ends by telling us to glorify God through "worship." While singing praise is a common way to worship God, we can worship God in many other ways. Any time we praise God, we are worshipping God. Anytime we acknowledge God for any of His attributes, we are worshipping God. Anytime we bow down to God and submit to Him as a creature before our creator, we are worshipping God. We glorify God by loving God with all our being, in every action we take, in every word we speak, and in every thought we have. Jesus stressed this importance when He explained that the most important command is, "Hear, O Israel: The Lord our God, the Lord is one. And you shall love the Lord your God with all your heart and with all your soul and with all your mind and with all your strength."[5]

---

[2] The first five chapters of Leviticus are all about the law for different offerings: Burnt Offerings, Grain Offerings, Peace Offerings, Sin Offerings, and Guilt Offerings.
[3] Hebrews 10:10, 14.
[4] Hebrews 13:15-16.
[5] Mark 12:29-30.

PURPOSE OF LIFE

Why is glorifying God so important? Why is this the foundation of being a Disciple of Christ?

Psalm 148 explains that God created all things (the heavens, the earth, the sun, the moon, the sky, the sea, mountains, trees, fire, snow, birds, fish, beasts, bugs, and all people on the earth) for one united purpose.[6] Now, each piece of creation has their own specific purpose, but all of creation was created with the same primary purpose. Think about that: the primary purpose of life for mankind is the same purpose as a bug, a tree, and a rock. What could be the shared purpose of all these vastly different parts of creation? Psalm 148 gives us our answer by stating, "Let them praise the name of the LORD, for His name alone is exalted; His majesty is above earth and heaven."[7] In fact, the phrase "Praise the LORD" or "Praise Him" is stated twelve times within this fourteen verse Psalm. After reading this Psalm you cannot help but conclude that the purpose of all creation is to "Praise the LORD!"

Why should we glorify God? Why is He alone worthy of all praise? Psalm 148 answers this question as well, stating, "Let them praise the name of the LORD! For He commanded and they were created."[8] God is the creator of all things and that alone is reason to give glory to God. This purpose is explicitly stated by God through the prophet Isaiah that, "everyone who is called by my name, *whom I created for my glory*, whom I formed and made."[9] God clearly reveals to Isaiah that all that He formed and made was created for His glory. Therefore, creation was created to glorify God.[10]

---

[6] Psalm 148 is my favorite Psalm. While I will quote two key verses from this Psalm, I encourage you to look up the Psalm to read it in its entirety.

[7] Psalm 148:13.

[8] Psalm 148:5.

[9] Isaiah 43:7, emphasis mine.

[10] Thank you, God, for creating me; thank you for giving me life!

Since God is the creator, He gives us our purpose. Just as an inventor creates an invention with an intended purpose, God created us with an intended purpose. Therefore, we can only find the purpose of life in Him. He created us for His glory, therefore the purpose of life is to glorify God.

Furthermore, glorifying God is an eternal purpose, it never ends. While exiled on the island of Patmos, the Apostle John received a revelation from Christ about the end of times and the return of Christ. During this revelation, John saw a glimpse of the throne of God where he saw angelic creatures and twenty-four elders worshipping God with the following words:

"Holy, holy, holy,
is the Lord God Almighty,
who was and is and is to come."[11]

"Worthy are You, our Lord and God,
to receive glory and honor and power,
for You created all things,
and by Your will they existed and were created."[12]

Notice that in their worship, the heavenly host declare that God is worthy of glory and honor because He created all things, echoing the same reason found in Psalm 148. The psalmist, the angelic beings, and the twenty-four elders each recognized that their very existence is due to the power of God. Therefore, He alone is worthy to be glorified. John goes on to say that this worship goes on day and night. It never ends!

Yet, not only did God create us, but He also saved us. We all have sinned and in our sin we deserve death. However, Jesus came to rescue us from our doomed state;

---

[11] Revelation 4:8.
[12] Revelation 4:11.

therefore, we should glorify God for the salvation that He gave us in Christ. The Apostle John describes Jesus' coming in terms of seeing God's glory stating that, "the Word became flesh and dwelt among us, we have seen His *glory*, *glory* as of the only Son from the Father, full of grace and truth."[13] John celebrated Jesus' coming because Jesus is the incarnate God and thus is worthy of glory.[14]

Additionally, angels celebrated God's glory at Jesus' birth when they revealed to the shepherds in the field, stating, "for unto you is born this day in the city of David a Savior, who is Christ the Lord."[15] After sharing this news, the angels began to praise God by saying, "*Glory* to God in the highest, and on earth peace among those with whom He is pleased."[16] The angels gave glory to God to celebrate what Jesus came to do. Jesus is worthy of our glory because He is God in the flesh. Furthermore, He came to take the punishment that we deserved to give us a life that we did not earn. Glory be to God for His saving grace.

God's work of creation and salvation are each reason alone to praise, worship, and glorify Him. Yet, God's blessings and good graces do not stop there. Like an endless river, He continues to pour into us blessing after blessing. Every good thing that we see, every good thing that happens, every good thing that we feel, every good thing that we experience are all from God, for He is the author of every good thing.[17] As we reflect on the countless blessings that He has given us, it should remind us that He is our loving God who desires a genuine relationship with us. We glorify God in part to fulfill our created purpose, but also to

---

[13] John 1:14, emphasis mine.

[14] **Incarnation:** To become flesh. "The act of God the Son whereby he took to himself a human nature" (Grudem, *Systematic Theology*, 678).

[15] Luke 2:11.

[16] Luke 2:14, emphasis mine.

[17] James 1:17 states, "Every good gift and every perfect gift is from above, coming down from the Father of lights with whom there is no variation or shadow due to change."

demonstrate our love and appreciation for our loving God. Only He is worthy of all praise and glory since He alone is God.

"Make a joyful noise to the LORD, all the earth!
Serve the LORD with gladness!
Come into his presence with singing!
Know that the LORD, He is God!
It is He who made us, and we are His;
we are His people, and the sheep of His pasture.
Enter His gates with thanksgiving, and His courts with praise!
Give thanks to Him; bless His name!
For the LORD is good;
His steadfast love endures forever,
and His faithfulness to all generations."
~ Psalm 100

Chapter 2
Glory To Christ: God's Glory, Man's Sin

THE PROBLEM OF SIN

We were created by God to give glory to God. What happens when we do not live up to this purpose? What happens when we reject this purpose? This is the problem of sin. Sin is to rebel against God. To reject our purpose and refuse to glorify God is the ultimate form of our rebellion against God. When we refuse to glorify God, we reject our created purpose and therefore reject God.

Refusing to glorify God is the mother of all sins in that every sin is a form of glorifying something or someone other than God. God addresses this in His first commandment stating, "You shall have no other gods before me."[1] There is more to this command than just not believing in other gods. Rather, this command is getting to the heart of the issue by addressing who or what we worship. God stated to Isaiah, "I am the LORD; that is my name; my glory I give to no other, nor my praise to carved idols."[2] Only God is worthy of worship and glory. To worship anyone or anything other than God is to commit the sin of idolatry.

An idol is anything we worship in place of God. To regard anything as more important than God or to trust in something more than God is to worship that thing in place of God, as a functioning god in our life. Idols are often tangible things, such as: money, possessions, other people and ourselves. Additionally, idols are frequently intangible things as well, such as: entertainment, pleasure, love, or a sense of security. The way we spend our money and use our time can be an indicator of what we truly value (and for some "time" itself can be an idol). Notice that the examples listed

---

[1] Exodus 20:3.
[2] Isaiah 42:8.

are not in themselves bad or wrong, but they become an idol when we value or trust any of them (or anything else) more than God. To value something/someone more than God is to worship that thing/person in place of God. Each time that we sin, we are actively choosing something over God. When we sin, our actions are saying that the sin is more important than God. Therefore, when we commit any sin, we are worshipping and glorifying something other than God, using our created purpose against the One who created us.

When we sin, we are rebelling against God, who is the good and just Lord of all creation. Therefore, we condemn ourselves to a justly deserved death.

When we sin, we rebel against our creator, and therefore separate ourselves from the giver and sustainer of life, causing our own death.

When we sin, we rebel against the glory of God, and therefore go against our designed purpose. Do you see how this is self-defeating? Many of us search for the meaning of life in nearly every area of life beyond God; yet, our meaning can only be fulfilled when we dedicate our life to the glory of God. To seek for meaning elsewhere is meaningless and will eventually lead us to determine that life itself is without meaning. What happens to the person who concludes that there is no meaning to life or determines that there is no purpose to life?

I encourage you now to examine your own heart. Have you ever placed something above God? Have you ever made something else a higher priority? Have you ever done something that you were not supposed to do? Have you ever failed or refused to do something that you should have done? The hard truth is that we have all been infected and corrupted by sin and thus we all sin, "for all have sinned and fall short of the glory of God."[3] This sin goes deeper than these

---

[3] Romans 3:23, notice that this verse defines sin in terms of "falling short of the *glory* of God." Emphasis mine.

questions would even have us understand. All the questions that I asked at the beginning of this paragraph only highlight the symptoms of our sinful nature. The true problem, the root of sin, goes back to our heart. The sinful actions that we commit are just the fruit of our sinful heart. To address the fruit, we need to focus on the root.[4] The root problem is that we reject God, and our heart seeks to glorify something else other than God.

You may be thinking to yourself, "well, I may not be perfect, but I'm not *that* bad." These types of statements minimize sin. When we minimize sin, we try to escape from the guilt of sin in our minds. The issue is, regardless if we are able to convince ourselves that sin is no big deal, it does not dismiss the reality of the severity of sin. Every sin is a big deal because every sin is against an infinitely holy God.

Scripture tells us that "the wages of sin is death."[5] Two things are revealed about sin in this passage: First, notice that this is a blanket statement that covers all sin. It is not that only some sins are deserving of death, rather every sin is deserving of death. Since the root of every sin is ultimately about denying God's glory, then every sin is deserving of the same punishment: death. This means that there is no such thing as a "small" sin. Second, notice that the word "sin" in the passage is singular. This means that all it takes to deserve death is to commit one sin. To take that thought further, that means each time we sin we incur an additional death sentence against ourselves. Thus eternal damnation in hell is the just place for those who rebel against God.

Furthermore, attempting to rationalize or minimize our sin prevents us from repenting of our sin. A person who believes that their iniquities are no big deal will see no reason to repent of their transgressions, and therefore will have no

---

[4] The concept of tracing the fruit of the sin action to the root of the sinful heart is from the book *Gospel Fluency* by Jeff Vanderstelt.
[5] Romans 6:23.

conviction to embrace a Savior from their sins.[6] Just as it is only when we realize that we are sick that we seek treatment from a doctor, it is only when we realize that we are sinners that we will embrace the salvation offered to us from the Savior.

Perhaps you are thinking, "my non-believer friend does many great things for others, so they can't be that bad." These types of statements undermine the deeper issue of sin, which is refusing to give God glory. Scripture tells us that as sinners "all our righteous deeds are like a polluted garment."[7] God looks at what we consider good and righteous deeds as a gross mess, because if we are not doing them for the glory of God, then why are we doing them? Are we doing good deeds for someone else? Do we do them to serve an abstract idea? Do we do them for our own glory? If we do good and righteous deeds for something other than the glory of God, then we must be doing it for the glory of something else. If we do good and righteous deeds for the glory of something other than God, then we are glorifying something over God and therefore these so-called "good and righteous deeds" are sins.

If any work is not first and foremost for the glory of God then that "good work" is sin, even when we do a work that the world would consider good or even a work that Scripture says is good. God views the good works of a non-believer as a disgusting mess, because when people do good works for something other than Him, we are worshipping something other than Him. But only He is worthy of our worship. These worldly "good works" do not please God. They insult God. These "good works" are sins, as Scripture states, "for whatever does not proceed from faith is sin."[8]

---

[6] **Repentance:** Turning from sin and to turn to God. "A heartfelt sorrow for sin, a renouncing of it, and a sincere commitment to forsake it and walk in obedience to Christ" (Grudem, *Systematic Theology*, 865).

[7] Isaiah 64:6. A more accurate translation of "polluted garment" is a used menstrual rag.

[8] Romans 14:23.

We can only glorify God through faith in Christ. In fact, Scripture tells us that "without faith it is impossible to please Him."[9] Since God is only pleased by those who glorify Him in faith, it is impossible for non-believers to glorify God.

To clarify, God CAN use our sin for His glory. We frequently see God using our evil to serve His good throughout Scripture. An example of this is demonstrated in the book of Genesis when Joseph's brothers conspired against him, trapping him in a hole and then selling him to slavers. They had hatred in their hearts and meant to do evil against their brother. Little did they know that God would use their sin to place Joseph in a position to save Israel during a seven-year famine. When Joseph revealed himself to his brothers, his brothers feared Joseph because they knew that they had done evil to Joseph. Yet, Joseph demonstrates grace by stating, "Do not fear, for am I in the place of God? As for you, you meant evil against me, but God meant it for good, to bring it about that many people should be kept alive, as they are today."[10] This is a great demonstration of forgiveness and trust in God's plan even when evil occurs. Yet, let us not mistake Joseph's brothers' sinful actions as glorifying to God. Their actions did not glorify God, rather God used their actions for His glory.

The greatest example of God using our evil for His glory is the cross. It was evil and hate that led mankind to torture and crucify Jesus. Not only did mankind condemn an innocent man to death, but they killed the incarnate God. Can there be an action more sinful than killing God? Yet, God used our greatest act of evil for our greatest good. In Jesus' death, we are given forgiveness and a restored relationship with God. The people who crucified Jesus were not glorifying God when they killed Him, yet God used their sin for His glory. Even though God used this for the greatest good and for His glory, and even though Jesus willingly gave

---

[9] Hebrews 11:6.
[10] Genesis 50:19-20.

His life for us; the people who crucified Jesus were still called to repent for their sin.[11] God is not glorified by evil, yet He can use evil for His glory. This does not excuse the sin, rather it serves to demonstrate God's power and glory.

THE SOLUTION TO SIN

The Good News is that Jesus came to earth to redeem us from our sins. Without Jesus we would be doomed to death, separated from God, living a life without purpose, and destined to suffer in hell for all eternity. There is nothing that any of us could do to remedy this situation since we simply do not have the power, strength, or ability to atone for our own sins. We are helpless in our sins. Yet, in our helplessness, Jesus washed us of our sins. He did this out of love for us, desiring to have a relationship with us.

Jesus took the punishment of sin that we deserved, in so doing He offers us forgiveness. The punishment for sin is separation and death. On the cross, Jesus took our sins upon Himself and for the first time in eternity He experienced a separation from the Father. This separation caused Jesus to call out, "My God, my God, why have you forsaken me."[12] Jesus then died the death that we deserved to give us eternal life.

We now can enjoy a restored relationship with God. The punishment of our sin is paid for in full through Christ. The forgiveness that we have in Christ does not mean that we are now free to sin, and we may still experience natural

---

[11] Acts 2:36-39 states, "'Let all the house of Israel therefore know for certain that God has made Him both Lord and Christ, this Jesus whom you crucified.' Now when they heard this they were cut to the heart, and said to Peter and the rest of the apostles, 'Brothers, what shall we do?' And Peter said to them, 'Repent and be baptized every one of you in the name of Jesus Christ for the forgiveness of your sins, and you will receive the gift of the Holy Spirit. For the promise is for you and for your children and for all who are far off, everyone whom the Lord our God calls to Himself.'"

[12] Matthew 27:46; cross reference with Mark 15:34 and Psalm 22:1.

consequences to our sin. But the eternal punishment for sin has been settled and now in our forgiveness we can enjoy our genuine relationship with God.

We did not and could not earn this forgiveness. Again, our good works are like a dirty rag that only makes the mess worse, thus it is impossible for our so-called "good works" to have any atoning value. We are only saved because God, full of grace, chose to save us. Salvation cannot be earned. Rather we can only receive this salvation through faith in Christ. Scripture states, "for by grace you have been saved through faith. And this is not of your own doing; it is the gift of God, not a result of works, so that no one may boast."[13] Glory be to God that He did not leave us in our sin, but instead became flesh to redeem us from our sin by dying on the cross.

In the death and resurrection of Jesus, we have been forgiven, cleansed, and freed from sin. Jesus did this by taking all our sins upon Himself while on the cross and in exchange Jesus gave us His righteousness. Scripture explains this exchange stating, "for our sake He made Him to be sin who knew no sin, so that in Him we might become the righteousness of God."[14] Do you see God's love for us? Not only did Jesus lay down his life to die a death that we deserved, but He bore the sins of mankind across all time in one moment while on the cross, none of which He committed for He was without sin. Can you imagine bearing the wrath of God for all your sins in one moment? We could not survive it. Yet, Jesus, who never sinned, voluntarily took upon Himself the sins of mankind throughout all time and suffered the severe consequences of those sins all at once to save us from the consequences that we deserve. And as amazing as that is, Christ's love for us did not stop there. He not only took our sins upon Himself, but then gave us His righteousness.

---

[13] Ephesians 2:8-9.
[14] 2 Corinthians 5:21.

This exchange is essential for our salvation because God is holy and we are not. Being full of sin, we could not withstand the presence of God, thus we had to be separated from God.[15] Furthermore, being separated from the giver and sustainer of life leads to death, a death justly deserved. Thankfully, Jesus did not just take our sins upon Himself, but He also gave us His righteousness and made us holy. Scripture explains the work of Christ by stating:

> "For in Him all the fullness of God was pleased to dwell, and through Him to reconcile to Himself all things, whether on earth or in heaven, making peace by the blood of His cross. And you, who once were alienated and hostile in mind, doing evil deeds, He has now reconciled in His body of flesh by His death, in order to present you holy and blameless and above reproach before Him."[16]

Since God is holy, we can only have a relationship with God through being clothed with the righteousness of Christ. In fact, the primary purpose of Jesus' death was to reconcile our relationship with God. Scripture tells us that "God has not destined us for wrath, but to obtain salvation through our Lord Jesus Christ, who died for us so that whether we are awake or asleep we might live with Him."[17] Notice the language in this passage describes salvation as the ability to

---

[15] Since the holiness of God cannot mix with sin, this separation is an act of grace, because if we were to encounter the presence of God in our sinful state we would immediately perish. We deserve immediate death the moment we sin; yet God, in His grace, separates Himself from us so that we may live a little longer and enjoy the beauty of His work. Theologians refer to this aspect of God's grace as common grace.
Common Grace: "The grace of God by which He gives people innumerable blessings that are not part of salvation" (Grudem, *Systematic Theology*, 803).
[16] Colossians 1:19-22.
[17] 1 Thessalonians 5:9-10.

live with God. This is relational language. Salvation and eternal life are ultimately about enjoying a genuine relationship with God.

In order to restore this relationship, Jesus died on the cross to take our sins and to clothe us with His righteousness. It is only when the work of sin is undone and our relationship restored that we are able to glorify God. Mankind, along with all of creation, was created to give glory to God. However, unlike the rest of creation, mankind was made in the image of God. God created us in His image because we were created to be His representatives within creation as stewards of the earth to take care of all that God created.[18] Therefore, unlike the rest of creation, we were created to have a special relationship with God. Thus, mankind was designed to glorify God through our unique relationship with Him.

However, when sin entered the world, our relationship with God was broken. Since our ability to glorify God is dependent on our relationship with Him, our fallen state put us in a position where we were not able to glorify God, as Scripture states, "those who are in the flesh cannot please God."[19] Furthermore, as sinners, we were children of wrath living in rebellion against God.[20] In our fallen state, we had no desire to glorify God as Scripture explains "none is righteous, no, not one; no one understands; no one seeks for God."[21]

---

[18] Genesis 1:27-28 states, "so God created man in His own image, in the image of God He created him; male and female He created them. And God blessed them. And God said to them, 'Be fruitful and multiply and fill the earth and subdue it, and have dominion over the fish of the sea and over the birds of the heavens and over every living thing that moves on the earth.'" Cross reference with Genesis 2:15.

[19] Romans 8:8.

[20] Ephesians 2:1-3 states, "And you were dead in the trespasses and sins in which you once walked, following the course of this world, following the prince of the power of the air, the spirit that is now at work in the sons of disobedience – among whom we all once lived in the passions of our flesh, carrying out the desires of the body and the mind, and were by nature children of wrath, like the rest of mankind."

[21] Romans 3:10-11.

Jesus' work of salvation is in direct response to the fallen state of the world and the sinful nature of mankind. In His death and resurrection, our relationship with God has been reconciled, which enables us to glorify God. Furthermore, by being clothed with the righteousness of Christ, Jesus' work redeems our heart by giving us a new heart and a new spirit, which gives us a desire to glorify Him.[22] Since the root of all sin is to deny God's glory and since Jesus died on the cross to redeem us from our sin, then it is only through Christ that we are able to rightly fulfill our created purpose of glorifying Him. In fact, Scripture states that we have received salvation "so that we who were the first to hope in Christ might be to the praise of His glory."[23] Therefore, there is a direct connection between the purpose of our creation (to glorify God) and the purpose of our salvation (to have a relationship with God).[24] Since we can only glorify God through our relationship with God, then the purpose of our salvation enables and drives us to fulfill the purpose of our creation.

---

[22] Ezekiel 36:26-27 states, "And I will give you a new heart, and a new spirit I will put within you. And I will remove the heart of stone from your flesh and give you a heart of flesh. And I will put my Spirit within you, and cause you to walk in my statutes and be careful to obey my rules."

[23] Ephesians 1:12.

[24] The answer to the first question of the Westminster Shorter Catechism makes this connection when it states, "Man's chief end is to glorify God, and to enjoy Him forever."

Chapter 3
Glory To Christ: The Transcendent Identity

RECEIVING A NEW IDENITY

Being a Disciple of Christ is about living a life in relationship with God. To the outside world this may look like doing good deeds and being a good person; but let us not overlook the underlying power of what produces the good works. Being a Disciple of Christ is more than just what we do or don't do. It is primarily about enjoying a genuine relationship with God. Since Jesus defines eternal life as knowing God, then the primary focus of the Christian is to have a relationship with God.[1] Furthermore, Scripture speaks of salvation in terms of enjoying a relationship with God, thus we are saved into a restored relationship.[2] As we grow in our relationship with Christ, we will do good works and we will strive to be a good person, however our relationship with God is not based on our works. These works and behaviors are simply a byproduct based on having genuine relationship with God.

Consider a married couple. Why does a husband do nice things for his wife? Why does a wife do nice things for her husband? Are they trying to earn each other's love? No, they are already married and already love each other. They do not do good works to earn the other's love. Rather, they do good works *because* they love each other. Likewise, Christians do not do good works to earn God's love. Rather, we do good works because of our love for God.

Christianity is more than a religion; it is a whole new identity that we have in Christ. Religion is a system of works

---

[1] John 17:3 states, "And this is eternal life, that they know you, the only true God, and Jesus Christ whom you have sent."

[2] 1 Thessalonians 5:9-10 states, "For God has not destined us for wrath, but to obtain salvation through our Lord Jesus Christ, who died for us so that whether we are awake or asleep we might live with Him."

that tells us how to please God and thus teaches that our works can earn a place with God. However, Christianity teaches us that our works cannot possibly earn salvation as they are like a dirty rag.[3] A dirty rag cannot clean up a mess; if anything, it just smears the mess and makes it worse. We are saved only by the work of Christ:

> "When the goodness and loving kindness of God our Savior appeared, He saved us, not because of works done by us in righteousness, but according to His own mercy, by the washing of regeneration and renewal of the Holy Spirit, whom He poured out on us richly through Jesus Christ our Savior."[4]

Therefore, good works cannot earn salvation, yet we are called to live good lives by glorifying God, thus we are called to do good works. Scripture explains the relationship between salvation and works by stating:

> "For by grace you have been saved through faith. And this is not your own doing; it is the gift of God, not a result of works, so that no one can boast. For we are His workmanship, created in Christ Jesus for good works, which God prepared beforehand, that we should walk in them."[5]

We are not saved by our works, rather we are saved to do good works. Good works does not produce salvation,

---

[3] Isaiah 64:6 states, "We have all become like one who is unclean, *and all our righteous deeds are like a polluted garment.* We all fade like a leaf, and our iniquities, like the wind, take us away." Emphasis mine.

[4] Titus 3:4-6.

[5] Ephesians 2:8-10. On a personal note, this is my second favorite passage in the Bible. As mentioned in a previous footnote, my favorite passage is John 17:3.

rather our salvation produces good works. We don't do good works to earn our place with God, rather we do good works *because* we are in relationship with God.[6] We do good works to show our appreciation for the many blessings God gives us each day, to demonstrate our love for Him, and ultimately to give Him glory.

When we examine this relationship between salvation and works, we see that good works is really a product of embracing our identity in Christ. God transforms us and changes who we are at our core by giving us His Spirit. God explained this work of transformation to the prophet Ezekiel stating:

> "And I will give you a new heart, and a new spirit I will put within you. And I will remove the heart of stone from your flesh and give you a heart of flesh. And I will put my Spirit within you, and cause you to walk in my statutes and be careful to obey my rules."[7]

As a Christian, the Holy Spirit dwells within you, gives you new life, and makes you a new creation. Thus, the Holy Spirit gives you a new identity in Christ.[8] While we are given this new identity from the moment we believe in Christ, the transforming work of the Holy Spirit will last a lifetime to conform you into the image of Christ.

---

[6] Philippians 2:13 states, "for it is God who works in you, both to will and to work for His good pleasure."

[7] Ezekiel 36:26-27.

[8] Romans 8:9-11, 29 states, "You, however, are not in the flesh but in the Spirit, if in fact the Spirit of God dwells in you. Anyone who does not have the Spirit of Christ does not belong to Him. But if Christ is in you, although the body is dead because of sin, the Spirit is life because of righteousness. If the Spirit of Him who raised Jesus from the dead dwells in you, He who raised Christ Jesus from the dead will also give life to your mortal bodies through His Spirit who dwells in you... For those whom He foreknew He also predestined to be conformed to the image of His Son, in order that He might be the firstborn among many brothers."

As a Christian, our identity is no longer a sinner, though we will still struggle with sin in this life. Jesus gives us a new identity in Him by clothing us with His righteousness. Therefore, Scripture repeatedly refers to all Christians as saints (one who is sanctified and holy). We have been sanctified by the blood of Christ, and therefore we have been made holy in Christ. In this new identity, Scripture calls us to "put off your old self, which belongs to your former manner of life and is corrupt through deceitful desires, and to be renewed in the spirit of your minds, and to put on the new self, created after the likeness of God in true righteousness and holiness."[9] Having our identity in Christ means that we share in His righteousness and are in full relationship with God.

Notice that our identity in Christ is applied to us both from inside-out and outside-in. He gives us new life and a new identity from the inside-out by placing His Spirit within us. But also, He covers us with the righteousness of Christ and thus our identity in Christ is applied outside-in.

As a Disciple of Christ, we should live out this identity in Christ in all that we do, starting with baptism. Baptism is the ceremony of embracing this new identity, which is why being baptized should be one of the first commands we follow. We see this command most explicitly stated in Jesus' departing words to His disciples:

> "All authority in heaven and on earth has been given to me. Go therefore and make disciples of all nations, baptizing them in the name of the Father and of the Son and of the Holy Spirit, teaching them to observe all that I have commanded you. And behold, I will be with you always, to the end of the age."[10]

---

[9] Ephesians 4:22-24; cross reference with Colossians 3:1-17.
[10] Matthew 28:18-20.

Notice that Jesus tells His disciples that one of the first things a new disciple should do is be baptized. When Peter first began preaching the gospel, he ended by saying, "Repent and be baptized everyone of you in the name of Jesus Christ for the forgiveness of your sins, and you will receive the gift of the Holy Spirit."[11] Therefore, one of the first commands a Disciple of Christ should obey is the command to be baptized.

At this point it should be clarified that baptism itself has no redeeming power. It does not wash our sins away, it does not give us new life, and it does not save us. To say that baptism does any of these things would make baptism a work that we must do to be saved, but we know that we are saved by faith alone. Furthermore, we know that it is only Jesus who washes away our sins, it is only God who gives us new life, and it is only through His work on the cross that we are saved. Baptism serves as a symbol to illustrate that our sins have been washed away, that we have been born again into a new life, and that we have been saved by Christ.

Why then are we commanded to be baptized? As mentioned, it is to embrace our identity in Christ. Scripture states, "for as many of you as were baptized into Christ have put on Christ. There is neither Jew nor Greek, there is neither slave nor free, there is no male and female, for you are all one in Christ Jesus."[12] As a Disciple of Christ, the only identity that should define us is our identity in Christ. When we are baptized, we are proclaiming that our identity in Christ will reign supreme over all that we are and all areas of our life. Baptism is a ceremony to outwardly express our inner faith in Christ, in which we glorify God by announcing our new identity to the world that we are Disciples of Christ!

---

[11] Acts 2:38.
[12] Galatians 3:27-28.

LIVING OUT OUR NEW IDENTITY

Our identity in Christ transcends beyond all other identities that we have. This is our primary identity, and it should affect all that we are and all that we do. No part of our life should be untouched by our identity in Christ. Rather, we should surrender all that we are to Christ.

For example, there are many "identities" that I have: I am a husband, a father, a soldier, and so on. However, my identity in Christ is a greater identity and should completely engulf all these areas. Therefore, my identity in Christ should dictate my heart as a husband, my identity in Christ should impact how I parent, and my identity in Christ should influence how I work. Overall, my identity in Christ should govern all that I do and all that I am.

Since the Disciple of Christ's primary purpose is to give glory to God and our identity in Christ governs every area of our lives, then giving glory to God should drive all that we do. Therefore, giving glory to God should be my focus when I am with my spouse. Giving glory to God should be my focus as I parent my child. Giving glory to God should be my focus when I am at work. Giving glory to God should be my focus when I watch a movie. Giving glory to God should be my focus when I drive my car (even in rush hour traffic). Scripture tells us, "so, whether you eat or drink, or whatever you do, do all to the glory of God."[13]

As Disciples of Christ, giving Him glory should be our primary focus in all that we do and in all areas of our lives. Since we are created to glorify God and we are saved into a relationship with God, then our life should reflect this restored relationship by dedicating our life to the glory of Christ. But this is not just a matter of duty; rather, glorifying God becomes a matter of who we are in Christ.

---

[13] 1 Corinthians 10:31.

We are to glorify God in everything that we do and everything we do should be for the glory of God. Glorifying God should be the driving factor of all that we are and all that we do. But what does this mean, what does this look like? Sure, it sounds nice to say, but how can we glorify God?

Timothy Keller answers this question in the New City Catechism[14] by stating, "we glorify God by enjoying Him, loving Him, trusting Him, and by obeying His will, commands and law."[15] Keller then quotes Scripture to reinforce this answer, "You shall therefore love the LORD your God and keep His charge, His statutes, His rules, and His commandments always."[16] It is important to again clarify, we do not obey God to earn His love (we cannot earn it), nor do we obey God to earn our salvation (we cannot earn it). Rather we obey God as an expression of our love for Him. We can trust in God's wisdom that all His commands are for our good and for His glory. Therefore, we demonstrate this trust by obeying His commands in love, recognizing that He is God and we are not. When we lovingly obey His commands, we recognize that He is our all-knowing, all-powerful, loving creator, and we are His creation, created to give Him glory.

We can glorify God in the simple everyday actions by praising Him and recognizing His glory in all that we do. Yet this is not always easy. Our hearts are quickly distracted with things other than the glory of God. If we find ourselves not glorifying God in what we are doing, then this means that either the action itself is a sin or that our heart needs to be realigned in conducting the action. We distinguish between these two types of actions because failure to glorify God in

---

[14] **Catechism:** A method of teaching using a series of questions and answers.
[15] New City Catechism, Question 6: How can we glorify God?
[16] Deuteronomy 11:1.

our actions does not necessarily mean that the action itself is a sin.

For example, I can drive my vehicle in a way that glorifies God or in a way that does not glorify God. The action of driving a car is not a sin. If I recognize that I am not glorifying God in my driving, then I need to repent of my sin of not glorifying God and then my heart needs to be realigned to glorify God in my driving. It is not that I need to abstain from driving, I simply need an alignment check on my heart.

Whereas stealing is a sin in and of itself. If I steal, then I need to repent of my sin by seeking God's forgiveness for valuing something higher than Him and for breaking His commands. In this case, part of repenting also means returning what I stole and abstaining from stealing in the future. We cannot glorify God in our sin, since the root of sin is to deny God's glory. Therefore, when we repent, we cannot continue in the sinful action.

Regardless if the action itself is a sin or not, if we are not glorifying God in what we are doing, our first response must be to repent of our sin of not glorifying God.

We are to give glory to God in all situations. Scripture tells us to, "rejoice in the Lord always; again I will say, rejoice."[17] Since giving glory is a matter of who we are in Christ, then we are able to glorify God in all circumstances. Whether things are good or bad we are to rejoice and glorify God. The importance of this truth is explored in the books of Ecclesiastes and Job.[18]

In the book of Ecclesiastes, King Solomon explores the meaning of life. King Solomon was one of the wealthiest, most powerful, and one of the wisest kings of all time. He was a man who had it all and attempted to find meaning in all that he had. However, after searching for the meaning of

---

[17] Philippians 4:4.
[18] Job is pronounced with a long O, rhymes with robe.

life in knowledge, wisdom, pleasure, self-indulgence, work, and wealth, he concludes that all of it is meaningless stating, "vanity of vanities, says the Preacher, vanity of vanities! All is vanity."[19] He concludes the book stating that only worshipping God has meaning, nothing else really matters. Ecclesiastes is a story of a man who has it all and concludes that the only thing that has meaning is to glorify God.

We see this truth echoed in the book of Job but from the opposite spectrum. Job is a man who loses his property, livestock, and fortune to raiding parties of other nations. Then his children are killed in a storm and eventually he suffers from an illness that gives him sores from head to toe. Through all of this, Job's initial response is to glorify God, stating, "The LORD gave, and the LORD has taken away; blessed be the name of the LORD."[20] The book then focuses on his time of mourning with three unhelpful friends and the book concludes with Job worshipping God. Job is a story of a man who loses it all and concludes that the only thing that has meaning is to glorify God.

When we look at Solomon and Job back to back, we have a man who has it all and a man who loses it all and they both conclude that the meaning of life is to glorify God. Therefore, we can conclude that whether we have it all, lose it all, or somewhere in between, we are to glorify God. Admittedly, this is easier said than done. Sometimes life gets hard. Sometimes people we encounter are challenging. Sometimes our own temptations and sinful nature get the better of us. During these times it is all the more important to cling to our identity in Christ and turn to Him.

Scripture encourages us to "fight the good fight of the faith. Take hold of the eternal life to which you were called and about which you made the good confession in the presence of many witnesses."[21] There may be times that we

---

[19] Ecclesiastes 1:2.
[20] Job 1:21.
[21] 1 Timothy 6:12.

feel like we are fighting an uphill battle. Yet, regardless of what happens in this world, nothing is greater than the gift of the eternal life that we have received in Christ. Nothing else should define us. We are able to "fight the good fight" when we embrace our identity in Christ.

Let us always glorify God in all that we do, even if we do not really enjoy what we are doing or perhaps we don't enjoy the people we are working with (such as a supervisor or coworker). Maybe we have a hard time finding meaning in our work, or even think that our work doesn't really matter. To that I say you are right, our work does not have meaning… if not done for the glory of God. However, when done for the glory of God, then it has significant meaning (regardless of what it is). Therefore, the problem is not with the work, nor is it the people you work with; the problem is with the heart.

As a Disciple of Christ, we need to realign our heart to give glory to God through our work. However, we can only do this when we embrace our identity in Christ and recognize that "whatever you do, work heartily, as for the Lord and not for men, knowing that from the Lord you will receive the inheritance as your reward. You are serving the Lord Christ."[22] In our identity in Christ, we are servants of the Lord and everything that we do should be for His glory.

Sometimes we get caught up in what is temporary and need to remember that which is of eternal importance. Scripture reminds us to embrace our identity in Christ, stating:

> "If then you have been raised with Christ, seek the things that are above, where Christ is seated at the right hand of God. Set your minds on things that are above, not on things that are on earth. For you have died, and your

---

[22] Colossians 3:23-24.

life is hidden with Christ in God. When Christ who is your life appears, then you also will appear with Him in glory."[23]

Therefore, let us always look to Christ during the good times, during the bad times, and everything in between. He created us and saved us and no power on earth can undo the reality of this eternal gift. Our identity in Christ should impact all areas of our life; therefore, all thoughts, words, and actions should be based on our relationship with God and for His glory. Our identity in Christ is a great gift; not just in our salvation, but in whom we have become in Christ. In our identity in Christ, God has bestowed upon us many blessings and equipped us with many gifts, therefore let us use those gifts to the glory of Him who provided them. Let us remember Peter's words:

"As each has received a gift, use it to serve one another, as good stewards of God's varied grace: whoever speaks, as one who speaks oracles of God, whoever serves, as one who serves by the strength that God supplies – in order that in everything God may be glorified through Jesus Christ. To Him belong glory and dominion forever and ever. Amen."[24]

---

[23] Colossians 3:1-4.
[24] 1 Peter 4:10-11.

GLORY TO CHRIST
PURPOSE, RELATIONSHIP, & IDENTITY

G
L
O
R
Y

"So, whether you eat or drink, or whatever you do, do all to the GLORY of God."
~1 Corinthians 10:31

- What does it mean to do all for the glory of God? What would your life look like if everything you did was for the glory of God? How does God's glory define your identity?
- What else in this world competes for God's glory? What things are you tempted to glorify over God? What things do you place in your heart as more important than God?
- Why is God, and God alone, worthy of all glory?

*** PAUSE HERE TO PRAYFULLY REFLECT ON THE ABOVE PASSAGE & QUESTIONS***

PART II
GROW IN CHRIST

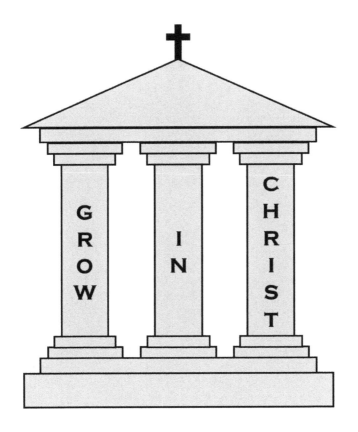

"Rather, speaking the truth in love, we are to **GROW** up in every way into Him who is the head, into Christ."
~ Ephesians 4:15

Chapter 4
Grow In Christ: Transformational Calling

CYCLE OF GROWTH

As Disciples of Christ, we are called to grow in Christ. We are to grow in Christ in two main areas: we are to grow in our relationship with Christ and we are to grow in our identity in Christ (that is to become more like Christ). Both our relationship with Christ and our identity in Christ are given to us the moment we have faith in Christ. However, we will continue to grow in this relationship and in our identity for the rest of our life.

Furthermore, we see a direct correlation between these two areas. Since our identity in Christ is rooted in our relationship with Christ, then as we grow in our relationship with Christ we will grow in our identity in Christ. As we grow in our identity in Christ, we grow in His likeness and as image bearers of His glory. As we grow to be more like Christ, we grow in our understanding of His truth, love, and glory. As we grow in our understanding of Christ's truth, love, and glory, we grow in our appreciation of Him and embrace Him all the more; thus, we grow in our relationship with Christ. A Disciple of Christ continues in this cycle of growth for their entire life.

The life of a Disciple of Christ is a journey where God makes us holy and transforms us to be more like Christ, as Scripture states, "for those whom He foreknew He also predestined to be *conformed to the image of His Son*."[1] Each disciple may be on a different part of this journey, but we are all on the same journey where we are being transformed into Christlikeness. Therefore, we should encourage and help each other as we continue to grow into our identity in Christ.

CALL TO REPENTANCE

We each began this life as a sinner in rebellion against God, deserving death and hell. The second chapter of Ephesians makes this point by stating:

> "And you were dead in the trespasses and sins in which you once walked, following the course of this world, following the prince of the power of the air, the spirit that is now at work in the sons of disobedience – among whom we all once lived in the passions of our flesh, carrying out the desires of the body and the mind, and were by nature children of wrath, like the rest of mankind."[2]

Yet, as an enemy of God, God called us into relationship with Him. The second chapter of Ephesians goes on to say, "but God, being rich in mercy, because of the great love with which He loved us, even when we were dead in our trespasses, made us alive together with Christ- by grace you have been saved."[3] God's love for us is more powerful than any transgression and therefore overcomes any sin. In His

---

[1] Romans 8:29, emphasis mine.
[2] Ephesians 2:1-3.
[3] Ephesians 2:4-5.

love, God calls us to enjoy a genuine relationship with Him. He made this relationship possible by forgiving our transgressions through the cross of Jesus. However, while God calls us in our sins, He does not call us to stay in our sins. Rather, He calls us to turn away from our sin as we follow Him. We are to repent of our transgressions by turning away from our sins and turning to Christ. Scripture reminds us that "at one time you were darkness, but now you are light in the Lord. Walk as children of light."[4] As a Disciple of Christ, we should not continue to walk as if we are still in darkness. Remember, sin is to rebel against God, the result of which separates us from God and leads to death. However, Jesus died the death we deserved for the sins that we committed so that we could enjoy a genuine relationship with God for all eternity.

When we embrace this truth and taste the good news of the gospel, how can we continue in our rebellion against Him? If we repent and turn to Jesus as our Lord and Savior, how can we continue in our sin? Let us remember Jesus' words, "Why do you call me 'Lord, Lord,' and not do what I tell you?"[5] Do you hear the hypocrisy that He is addressing? The frustration in His voice? How can we call ourselves Disciples of Christ and refuse His teachings? How can we call Him King and refuse His commands? How can we continue to rebel against Him who saved us? As a Disciple of Christ, we cannot stay in our sins. In fact, Scripture tells us that "we know that everyone who has been born of God does not keep on sinning."[6]

---

[4] Ephesians 5:8.
[5] Luke 6:46.
[6] 1 John 5:18.

TWO NATURES AND THREE ASPECTS

So why do Disciples of Christ, who have been "born of God," continue to struggle with sin?[7] There is a unique dichotomy in the identity of a Disciple of Christ. At the cross Jesus took our sins and in exchange gave us His righteousness. Therefore, our identity is no longer that of a sinner, rather our new identity is found in Christ. God has declared us righteous and freed us from our captivity to sin.[8] Furthermore, God did not just declare us righteous, He also gave us His Spirit to dwell within us. The indwelling Spirit gives us a new spiritual nature to transform our hearts to conform us "to the image of His Son."[9]

Yet, though declared righteous, we still have a sinful nature lingering within us, which is why we still struggle with sin, even as Disciples of Christ. Therefore, as Disciples of Christ, we exist with two natures, a sinful nature and a spiritual nature.[10] Peter describes these two natures as being at war within us.[11] Paul describes this internal conflict by writing that, "the desires of the flesh are against the Spirit, and the desires of the Spirit are against the flesh, for these are opposed to each other, to keep you from doing the things you want to do."[12] While we may struggle with this internal conflict, we can be comforted in knowing that the war has already been won. By the blood of Christ we have been set

---

[7] The concepts of "Two Natures" and "Three Aspects" are from a book called *Survival Kit: Five Keys to Effective Spiritual Growth* by Bill Latham and Ralph W. Neighbour.

[8] However, we must never forget that the righteousness in which we are declared is not our own.

[9] Romans 8:29 states, "For those whom He foreknew He also predestined to be conformed to the image of His Son, in order that He might be the firstborn among many brothers."

[10] Martin Luther described the two natures of the Christian by using the Latin phrase "simul iustus et peccator," which means "simultaneously justified and sinner."

[11] 1 Peter 2:11 states, "Beloved, I urge you as sojourners and exiles to abstain from the passions of the flesh, which wage war against your soul."

[12] Galatians 5:17.

free from sin.[13] By the power of the Holy Spirit we can overcome our temptations, thus we are told to "walk by the Spirit, and you will not gratify the desires of the flesh."[14]

Through Christ, God has declared us righteous and at the same time He is transforming us into His righteousness through the power of the indwelling Holy Spirit. This transformation does not happen all at once. In fact, as a Disciple of Christ this transformation will take place throughout our entire life. The apostle Paul explains this transformational work of God in our life by stating, "I am sure of this, that He who began a good work in you will bring it to completion at the day of Jesus Christ."[15] This passage shares an interesting perspective of salvation. Paul introduces the topic in this verse by stating that Jesus began a good work in us. Notice the language is past tense, Jesus did something in the past that began a good work. Of course, Paul is referring to the fact that Jesus died on the cross for our sins. Theologians refer to this past tense aspect of salvation as *justification*.[16] This theological term refers to the fact that Jesus took our sins upon Himself on the cross and paid the penalty of those sins so that the wrath of God would be satisfied. On the cross Jesus exchanged our sins with His righteousness. In our justification we are declared righteous and therefore saved from the penalty of sin.

However, notice that the passage continues to say that Jesus "will bring it [referring to the good work of salvation] to completion." Paul is stating that the work of salvation is not yet complete! This may be alarming to some, but rest assured that though the passage refers to the completion of

---

[13] Romans 6:6-7 states, "We know that our old self was crucified with Him in order that the body of sin might be brought to nothing, so that we would no longer be enslaved to sin. For one who has died has been set free from sin."

[14] Galatians 5:16.

[15] Philippians 1:6.

[16] **Justification:** "An instantaneous legal act of God in which he (1) thinks of our sins as forgiven and Christ's righteousness as belonging to us, and (2) declares us to be righteous in his sight" (Grudem, *Systematic Theology*, 885).

salvation in the future tense, we can fully trust that Jesus will in fact bring it to completion. Notice that Paul was able to open this sentence by stating, "And I am sure of this..."

The work has already been done, yet the result of this work will be made complete sometime in the future. Theologians refer to this future aspect of salvation as *glorification*.[17] This word refers to how Jesus will give us new glorified bodies, perfect and untouched by sin. Paul explains this aspect of salvation stating, "our citizenship is in heaven, and from it we await a Savior, the Lord Jesus Christ, *who will transform our lowly body to be like His glorious body*, by the power that enables Him even to subject all things to Himself."[18] Glorification is the completion of the transformational work of God. This will happen at the "day of Jesus Christ" referring to the end of times when Jesus returns. At this time, all evil and sin will be no more, our sinful nature will be vanquished. In our glorification, we will be saved from the presence of sin.

As Disciples of Christ, we are currently living in the times between the times, where we have been declared holy, yet we are not completely without sin. We are presently living in a time where we are being transformed into Christ's righteousness. Therefore, we exist with two natures because we are currently in the middle of this transformational process in which we are being made holy. During our transformation, we will have both ups and downs as we struggle with temptation. There will even be times when we succumb to sin. However, with the work of the Holy Spirit dwelling within us, we will continue to grow to be more like Christ. Theologians refer to this present tense aspect of

---

[17] **Glorification:** "The final step in the application of redemption. It will happen when Christ returns, raises from the dead the bodies of all believers for all time who have died, and reunites them with their souls, and changes the bodies of all believers who remain alive, thereby giving all believers at the same time perfect resurrection bodies like His own" (Grudem, *Systematic Theology*, 1018).

[18] Philippians 3:20-21, emphasis mine.

salvation as *sanctification*.[19] Sanctification is derived from the word sanctify, which means to be made holy. Therefore, the term "sanctification" focuses on the transformational process in which we are being made holy and refers to the transforming work of God to make us more like Christ. Sanctification is the journey of the Christian life where we are being saved from the power of sin.[20]

Aspects of Salvation			
Justification	Past Tense Aspect	Saved from	the PENALTY of sin
Sanctification	Present Tense Aspect	Being saved from	the POWER of sin
Glorification	Future Tense Aspect	Will be saved from	the PRESENCE of sin

Disciples of Christ begin their journey when we first truly trust in Jesus as our Lord, God, and Savior who declared us righteous by dying for our sins (justification) and this transformational journey of sanctification will end when we are made perfectly righteous in Christ (glorification). Therefore, as a Disciple of Christ, we will spend the remainder of this life struggling between our sinful nature and a spiritual nature as we continue to grow in Christ.

Pastor Mark Driscoll explains the three aspects of salvation by stating:

> "It is helpful to understand that though we are positionally righteous before God in Christ (have been saved), we may also struggle with sin because we are being made new and like Christ daily (are being saved). But we have

---

[19] **Sanctification:** "A progressive work of God and believers that makes us more and more free from sin and like Christ in our actual lives" (Grudem, *Systematic Theology*, 924).

[20] Relating justification, sanctification, and glorification in terms of having been saved from the penalty of sin, being saved from the power of sin, and will be saved from the presence of sin is from the book *Who Do You Think You Are? Finding Your True Identity in Christ* by Mark Driscoll.

hope, as Christians, that one day we will be perfect like Christ (shall be saved). The best part is, the past, present, and future work of salvation in our lives is all the work of Christ in us. Along every step of salvation, we are brought along by Jesus and lovingly empowered by his Holy Spirit."[21]

THE ROLE OF THE HOLY SPIRIT

While all three members of the Trinity play a role in our sanctification, our spiritual growth is primarily the role of the Holy Spirit. As Disciples of Christ, God gave us His Spirit to dwell inside each of us, as Scripture states:

"In Him you also, when you heard the word of truth, the gospel of your salvation, and believed in Him, were sealed with the promised Holy Spirit, who is the guarantee of our inheritance until we acquire possession of it, to the praise of His glory."[22]

Before we examine the implications of this indwelling Spirit, let us reflect on this great gift that God has bestowed upon us. The Holy Spirit is not some power that God has given us, nor is He an impersonal force that we may use and manipulate to our will. The Holy Spirit is the third person of the Trinity and therefore is God. As a Disciple of Christ, we have God dwelling in us! How amazing is that? As a Disciple of Christ, God lives inside you, He lives in me! Being a Disciple of Christ is about having a personal relationship with God, and it does not get more personal than God dwelling within you.

---

[21] Driscoll, *Who Do You Think You Are?*, 69.
[22] Ephesians 1:13-14.

There are many reasons that the Holy Spirit was sent to dwell inside us. First, He came to be our guarantee that we have been saved from our sins; therefore, we can be comforted in an assurance of our salvation.

Furthermore, when Jesus speaks of the coming Holy Spirit to His disciples, He tells them, "I will ask the Father, and He will give you another Helper, to be with you forever, even the Spirit of truth, whom the world cannot receive, because it neither sees Him nor knows Him. You know Him, for He dwells with you and will be in you."[23] Later in this conversation, Jesus goes on to say, "but the Helper, the Holy Spirit, whom the Father will send in my name, He will teach you all things and bring to your remembrance all that I have said to you."[24] Notice two things in Jesus' statements:

(1) Jesus consistently refers to the Holy Spirit as "He" and "Him" reinforcing that the Holy Spirit is a person and not an "it."

(2) Jesus also consistently refers to the Holy Spirit as "the Helper." This title refers to another reason that the Holy Spirit dwells inside each Disciple of Christ: He is to be our guide in our transformational journey, to help us overcome obstacles and temptations, and empower our growth in Christ.

As we reflect on the role of the indwelling Holy Spirit, let us remember that it is through the Holy Spirit that we were initially transformed into our new identity in Christ at the beginning of our journey.[25] Yet, the Holy Spirit does not just cause the initial transformation. He stays within us to sustain and nurture our transformational growth into this identity.

---

[23] John 14:16-17.
[24] John 14:26.
[25] This topic was explored in more detail in Chapter 3.

Chapter 5
Grow In Christ: Growing Pains

CHRISTIAN SUFFERING

The life of a Disciple of Christ will be a life of growth and transformation, but how does this growth occur and what does it look like in our life? The truth is this transformation is not always comfortable. In fact, we will experience something similar to growing pains in our spiritual growth. James explains these spiritual growing pains by stating, "count it all joy, my brothers, when you meet trials of various kinds, for you know that the testing of your faith produces steadfastness."[1] In this passage, James informs the church that our times of hardship and suffering will make us strong. He is not speaking of physical strength, rather in terms of spiritual fitness. Suffering produces spiritual growth.

Peter then describes how these times of hardship produce growth by explaining:

> "In this you rejoice, though now for a little while, if necessary, you have been grieved by various trials, so that the tested genuineness of your faith – more precious than gold that perishes though it is tested by fire – may be found to result in praise and glory and honor at the revelation of Jesus Christ."[2]

Notice that both James and Peter tell us to rejoice in our trials because they help us grow. Peter goes on to give a little further detail by explaining that our times of hardship will result in further praise, glory, and honor to Christ.

---

[1] James 1:2-3.
[2] 1 Peter 1:6-7.

When we experience suffering, we can appreciate Christ's suffering on the cross even more, which will cause us to have more appreciation and amazement of His love for us. This increased gratitude will naturally lead us to desire to grow in our relationship with Him who suffered on our behalf. Not only does suffering help us grow in our relationship with Christ, but it also helps us grow as image bearers of Christ.

Notice that Peter uses the imagery of gold being tested by fire. Peter is stating that our times of hardship have a similar purpose to a refiner's fire, which is used to purify gold. Chunks of ore would be placed in fire to remove the impurities. While the gold in the ore would be under a significant amount of heat, the gold itself would not be damaged. On the contrary, it would come out better than before. In fact, goldsmiths would continue to refine gold using this method until they could see a perfect reflection of themselves from the gold. By using this analogy, Peter is explaining that God uses times of hardship to refine Disciples of Christ so that we are better reflections of His image.[3]

Unfortunately, there is a perception by many Disciples of Christ that life gets easier once they embrace Christ. This is often due to flawed evangelical efforts which attempt to make Christianity as appealing as possible. However, this faulty technique of evangelism ends up emphasizing the great blessings associated with becoming a Disciple of Christ, but it refuses to mention anything that could be construed as negative.

There are many problems with this evangelical approach. First and foremost, it places the focus on man, not on God's

---

[3] Peter is likely referencing Malachi 3:2-3, "But who can endure the day of His coming, and who can stand when He appears? For He is like a refiner's fire and like fullers' soap. He will sit as a refiner and purifier of silver, and He will purify the sons of Levi and refine them like gold and silver, and they will bring offerings in righteousness to the LORD."

glory. Furthermore, it is deceptive and leaves new Disciples of Christ unprepared (and surprised) when life becomes hard.[4] This lie can lead these new Disciples of Christ down a dark path of doubt in their faith. Some could mistakenly view their time of suffering as a sign that they are doing something wrong, that they do not have enough faith, or are not doing enough (this quickly becomes works-based thinking). Some may even view the times of suffering as a testimony that Christianity is not true since it did not deliver the promised prosperity.

Therefore, Disciples of Christ should be taught to expect suffering, trials, and times of hardship in this life. Peter tells us to "not be surprised at the fiery trial when it comes upon you to test you, as though something strange were happening to you. But rejoice insofar as you share Christ's sufferings, that you may also rejoice and be glad when His glory is revealed."[5]

Becoming a Disciple of Christ is like putting on a military uniform and then crossing into enemy lines. We are warned that the enemy is on the prowl, and is ready to steal, kill, and destroy.[6] Satan desires that none would follow God and he will do everything in his power to make us wish we never embraced Christ.

Along with spiritual warfare, we also endure persecution from the world. Jesus frequently told His disciples that the world would hate them just for being a Disciple of Christ. Once we become a Disciple of Christ we are no longer of the world, and the world hates us for it.[7]

Not only do we suffer outward attacks against us once we become Disciples of Christ, but we may also experience suffering due to our own sinful nature. As a Disciple of

---

[4] Life may even become harder as a Disciple of Christ.

[5] 1 Peter 4:12-13.

[6] John 10:10 states, "The thief comes only to steal and kill and destroy. I came that they may have life and have it abundantly."

[7] John 17:14 states, "I have given them Your word, and the world has hated them because they are not of the world, just as I am not of the world."

Christ, we are fighting a war within ourselves. Our sinful nature desires things that are against us. Before we were a Christian, we were indulging our sinful nature by living out many of our sinful desires. As a Disciple of Christ, we are to give up the sinful actions that we use to do and think. Ultimately, we are called to give our whole life to Jesus. When Jesus evangelized, He was up front about all these "negative" aspects of being a Disciple of Christ and told people, "If anyone would come after me, let him deny himself and take up his cross daily and follow me."[8]

Therefore, as Disciples of Christ, we can expect to experience suffering from the enemy, from the world, and from our own sinful nature. However, we know that God can use all things for His glory. When we experience times of hardship, suffering, and sacrifice we can be comforted in knowing that these times can be used for our growth in Christ.

JOY IN SUFFERING

We will experience suffering as a Disciple of Christ. But ironically, the suffering we experience is not a downside. Scripture states, "for it has been granted to you that for the sake of Christ you should not only believe in Him but also suffer for His sake."[9] Notice the language used in this passage. Paul told the Philippians that it had been "granted" to them that they would suffer for Jesus, as if to say that it is an honor. Indeed, as strange as it may sound, it is a great privilege. When we suffer for Christ, we become witnesses to Christ, we become closer to Christ, we learn to trust and depend on Christ, and it nurtures our growth in becoming more like Christ.

So, no, life does not become easier when we become a Disciple of Christ, but it does become better. These times of

---

[8] Luke 9:23.
[9] Philippians 1:29.

suffering and hardship are insignificant when compared to the great blessings that we have in Christ. Let us consider Paul's words when he taught that "the sufferings of this present time are not worth comparing with the glory that is to be revealed to us."[10] To be sure, we do receive great blessings when we place our faith in Christ. First and foremost, we are given the grace of God which in turn grants us a true relationship with God. In our restored relationship, we are given eternal life, adopted as God's own sons and daughters, and receive an inheritance in the kingdom of God.

Furthermore, God has blessed us with the Holy Spirit who indwells within us to be our helper, comforter, and guide throughout the rest of our life. Being a Disciple of Christ means that we can have peace in the midst of war and chaos. Being a Disciple of Christ means that we have true joy in times of trial and suffering. Being a Disciple of Christ means that we can love in a world of hate. We have these blessings because the source of true joy and true peace and true love is from having a restored relationship with God and the indwelling power of the Holy Spirit.[11] Thanks be to Jesus for suffering on the cross and sacrificing His life to give us this most precious gift.

---

[10] Romans 8:18.

[11] Galatians 5:22-23 states, "But the fruit of the Spirit is love, joy, peace, patience, kindness, goodness, faithfulness, gentleness, self-control; against such things there is no law."

Chapter 6
Grow In Christ: The Pillars of Growth

SPIRITUAL TRAINING

While transformational growth in Christ is primarily the work of God working in us, we are not called to be passive objects in this growth. Rather Scripture calls us to take an active role stating, "train yourself for godliness; for while bodily training is of some value, godliness is of value in every way, as it holds promise for the present life and also for the life to come."[1] In this passage, Disciples of Christ are called to "train" themselves in "godliness." The term "godliness" refers to being like God. We should be holy as God is holy, loving as God is loving, and righteous as God is righteous. To say "train yourself for godliness" is simply another term to call us to grow in Christ. Therefore, we are called to train ourselves to be more like Christ.

When we train in an area, we are putting in effort to improve in that area. Therefore, this passage is calling us to put in effort for our spiritual growth. Notice that the passage compares this spiritual training to "bodily training." People who train their body, such as athletes, need to work out and eat right to train their body. With the same intensity and dedication that athletes train their bodies, Disciples of Christ are called to train for holiness by taking in spiritual nutrients to grow spiritually healthy. In fact, this passage states that our spiritual training should be even more important since our current bodily training is only of temporary value whereas our spiritual training holds eternal value. Certainly, something of eternal value should be held at a higher priority than something that only has temporary value.

So how do we train in godliness? How do we grow in Christ? Scripture tells us, "rather, **speaking the truth in**

---

[1] 1 Timothy 4:7-8; cross reference with Philippians 2:12-13 and 2 Peter 1:10.

61

love, we are to **grow** up in every way **into Him** who is the head, **into Christ,** from whom the whole body, joined and held together by every joint with which it is equipped, when each part is working properly, makes the body **grow** so that it builds itself up **in love.**"[2] This passage identifies two main sources that cause us to grow in Christ: truth and love.

The greatest declaration of truth and the greatest demonstration of love is found in the gospel. God, our creator in whom we rebelled against, came down as a man to die on the cross to redeem us from the punishment of our rebellion and restore our relationship with Him. There is no greater truth, for the truth of Christ is about our eternal relationship with the one true God. Furthermore, there is no greater demonstration of love than Jesus coming to die to save us while we were in open rebellion against Him. Jesus explicitly makes this point when He tells His disciples that "greater love has no one than this, that someone lay down his life for his friends."[3]

Since the gospel is about our restored relationship with God through Christ, then being a Disciple of Christ is about enjoying a restored relationship with God. Therefore, as we explore how we grow in Christ, we should look at how we can grow in our relationship with Christ. So, what makes a good relationship? What is essential to strengthen a relationship? The three key elements to any strong relationship are love, communication, and time together. We can apply these same principles to our relationship with God.

Love is the driving factor that encourages us to grow in our relationships. In fact, it was out of God's loving grace that Jesus came and died on the cross to restore our relationship. Therefore, it is due to God's love for us that we can enjoy a relationship with God.[4]

---

[2] Ephesians 4:15-16, emphasis mine.

[3] John 15:13; cross reference with John 10:11 and 1 John 3:16.

[4] Chapter 10 is dedicated to the role that love has in our growing relationship with God.

God communicates with us primarily through Scripture and we primarily communicate with God through prayer. Therefore, when we combine our Scripture reading with prayer, we are having a conversation with God. Furthermore, when we spend time in Scripture and prayer, we are spending time with God. We also spend time with God when we fellowship with other Disciples of Christ as Jesus explained, "for where two or three are gathered in my name, there am I among them."[5] Therefore, the three essential elements that nurture our growth and strengthen our relationship with Christ are Scripture, prayer, and fellowship.

Scripture, prayer, and fellowship do not only nurture our relationship with God, but they also provide spiritual nutrients that we need to grow in our identity in Christ. Just as our physical body needs food, water, and sleep to grow; we need Scripture, prayer, and fellowship for spiritual growth. What would happen to our body if we did not sleep, eat, or drink water? What would happen if we just stopped doing only one of them, but continued to do the other two?

Regardless of how much water we drink and how well we sleep, if we stopped eating, we would become fatigued and malnourished. Our body simply needs food to grow healthy.

If we eat healthy and get a full eight hours of sleep, but we stopped drinking water, we would become fatigued and dehydrated. Our body simply needs water to grow healthy.

If we had three balanced meals and drank plenty of water each day, but we stopped sleeping, we would become fatigued and our mind would break down. Our body simply needs sleep to grow healthy.

Food, water, and sleep are vital to our growth; not one can be ignored. If any of the three are neglected, we will become physically fatigued and ill. Similarly, Scripture,

---

[5] Matthew 18:20.

prayer, and fellowship are each vital to our spiritual growth; not one can be ignored without becoming spiritually fatigued.

They are the three Pillars of our Spiritual Growth.[6]

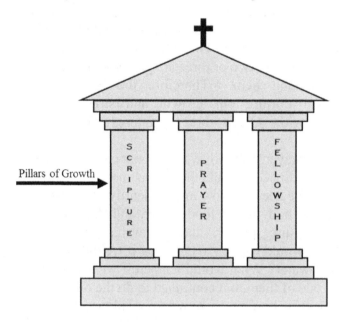

Pillars of Growth

THE SOURCE OF POWER

While we are called to "train [ourselves] for godliness,"[7] let us be comforted in the fact that ultimately God causes our growth. Paul reminds the church of Colossae to cling to Christ, "from whom the whole body, nourished and knit together through its joints and ligaments, grows with a growth that is from God."[8] To clarify, while this truth can certainly apply to our physical body, Paul is speaking metaphorically about our spiritual growth as a church body.

---

[6] The concept of the "Pillars of Growth" is based on teachings taught by Chaplain Jared Vineyard.

[7] 1 Timothy 4:7.

[8] Colossians 2:19.

Notice that he points to God as the causing factor for this growth, stating that "the whole body… grows with a growth that is *from* God." This truth is echoed in Paul's letter to the church at Corinth, where he explained the ministry of church planting by stating, "I planted, Apollos watered, but God gave the growth. So neither he who plants nor he who waters is anything, but only God who gives the growth."[9]

It is only through God that Scripture, prayer, and fellowship have the power to cause growth. Scripture, prayer, and fellowship are simply the power-tools that God uses to build our spiritual growth, but the thing about power-tools is that they only work when they have a source of power. In this case, God Himself is that source. It is the Holy Spirit dwelling in us that gives Scripture, prayer, and fellowship the power to cause growth.

---

[9] 1 Corinthians 3:6-7.

Chapter 7
Grow In Christ: The Pillar of Scripture

HEARING FROM GOD

As we begin reading Scripture, we will quickly notice that this book is like no other. It is a great tool that helps guide us throughout our lives. Paul writes in his second letter to Timothy that "all Scripture is breathed out by God and profitable for teaching, for reproof, for correction, and for training in righteousness, that the man of God may be complete, equipped for every good work."[1] In this letter, Paul tells his disciple that Scripture has many good uses and it equips us to walk through life as a Disciple of Christ. Everything that we need to know to walk a life with God is in this book. Furthermore, Scripture equips us to do "every good work" that God has called us to do.

But did you catch what makes Scripture so important? What makes it different from any other book out there? We will find our answer as we explore who authored the Bible. Scripture is actually a collection of writings from many different people: Moses, David, and Solomon are just some of the people who wrote the Old Testament; Paul, Luke, and John are just some of the people who wrote the New Testament. Yet, even though there were many people who wrote the Bible, there is actually only one author: God!

Before Paul explained the many ways that Scripture is useful, he first established something even more important, "all Scripture is breathed out by God." Scripture is much more than a useful tool that guides our lives, it is God's revelation about Himself and His will for us. The words written in the Bible are from God Himself.

Throughout time, God used different people to physically write His words and compile the Bible, yet God

---

[1] 2 Timothy 3:16-17.

is the author of all Scripture. Peter explained this process in his second letter to the church by stating "that no prophecy of Scripture comes from someone's own interpretation. For no prophecy was ever produced by the will of man, but men spoke from God as they were carried along by the Holy Spirit."[2] Every word of Scripture is from God written by men through the Holy Spirit. No word of Scripture was written by man's wisdom or will. These are God's very words. Reading Scripture is the primary way in which God speaks to us.

When we spend time in His word, we are spending time with God. As we spend time with God and hear His truth, we come to know Him better and grow in our relationship with Him. When we read Scripture, God is speaking into our lives and transforming our heart.

Scripture is the primary tool that God uses to conform us into the image of Christ. When we read Scripture, we will see how Christ speaks and acts, setting an example for us to follow. As we read Scripture, we see God's love and justice, which should be the standard for how we live. We should conform our lives according to the truths found in Scripture. In fact, the word of God penetrates our hearts and causes this transformation, "for the word of God is living and active, sharper than any two-edged sword, piercing to the division of soul and of spirit, of joints and of marrow, and discerning the thoughts and intentions of the heart."[3]

GOD SPEAKS TRUTH

Scripture is God's revealed truth to us. Therefore, we should use Scripture to measure any truth claim that we encounter throughout our lives. We see a great example of using Scripture to measure truth claims when Paul and Silas taught in the city of Berea. Before going to Berea, Paul and

---

[2] 2 Peter 1:20-21.
[3] Hebrews 4:12.

Silas had been preaching in the city of Thessalonica. While some in Thessalonica embraced Paul's teachings, there were others who were angered and started a mob to attack Paul and Silas. However, Paul and Silas were given a warning about the coming attack and were sent off by night to Berea. "When they arrived they went into the Jewish synagogue. Now these Jews were more noble than those in Thessalonica; they received the word with all eagerness, examining the Scriptures daily to see if these things were so."[4] Notice that the people of Berea were accepting of the gospel message presented to them by Paul, even EAGER to receive the Good News. However, they did not blindly accept Paul's teachings to be truth. Instead, they turned to the source of truth: Scripture. This should be an example to us all. Many people will attempt to give their two cents on what is truth; however, before accepting anyone's teaching, we should compare their teachings to Scripture.

Peter emphasizes the importance of trusting Scripture by stating:

> "For we did not follow cleverly devised myths when we made known to you the power and coming of our Lord Jesus Christ, but we were eyewitnesses of His majesty. For when He received honor and glory from God the Father, and the voice was borne to Him by the Majestic Glory, 'This is my beloved Son, with whom I am well pleased,' we ourselves heard this very voice borne from heaven, for we were with Him on the holy mountain. And we have the prophetic word more fully confirmed, to which you will do well to pay attention as to a lamp shining in a

---

[4] Acts 17:10-11.

dark place, until the day dawns and the morning star rises in your hearts."[5]

Peter was one of the first disciples of Jesus and had followed Him from the beginning of His ministry. He was one of three to witness Jesus' transfiguration up on the mountain. Peter was one of the few to see Jesus' empty tomb. He had been with Jesus multiple times after His resurrection. Yet, even after all that, Peter says that we have something better than his eyewitness account. We have "the prophetic word," referring to Scripture.

Just because someone claims to profess truth doesn't mean that they are speaking truth, for we know that there are false teachers and false spirits in this world. Sadly, many of these false teachers actually believe the lies that they teach and are all the more convincing. Thus, it is important to test what others proclaim to be true by comparing everything with Scripture.[6] Furthermore, we should apply this test to ourselves to ensure that what we believe and teach is in accordance to Scripture. We should not try to mold Scripture to fit our beliefs; rather, Scripture should mold what we believe.

When we recognize that Scripture is in fact God's words to us, we can trust it as authoritative (as God is the Lord of all Creation) and inerrant (as God is perfect). Therefore, we can trust the truths in Scripture as the highest source of authority in our lives and should obey His commands, knowing that His will is for His glory and our good.

---

[5] 2 Peter 1:16-19.

[6] 1 John 4:1 states, "Beloved, do not believe every spirit, but test the spirits to see whether they are from God, for many false prophets have gone out into the world."

THE HOLY SPIRIT EMPOWERS SCRIPTURE

Without the Holy Spirit, we would not be able to understand Scripture. Have you ever wondered why some can read Scripture and seem to get something out of it; while others can read the same passage and seem to get nothing out of it?

Scripture provides an example of this occurrence stating, "for the word of the cross is folly to those who are perishing, but to us who are being saved it is the power of God."[7] To clarify, the "word of the cross" refers to the gospel. This passage explains that non-believers reject the gospel as foolishness; while believers embrace the gospel as "the power of God." Why is it that some respond positively to the gospel while others dismiss or even rebuke it? Is it that the believer is smarter or wiser than the non-believer? Or is there something else going on?

When I would read the Bible prior to being a Disciple of Christ, the words did not mean much to me. While I intellectually understood the words that I read (more or less), I did not really comprehend them. They did not penetrate my heart, nor did I find them to be particularly impactful. During this time, I easily dismissed the truth of Scripture as either useful bits of wisdom at best or foolish nonsense at worst.[8]

But then one day, everything changed. God opened my mind to His truth and changed my heart to embrace His truth. Suddenly, I began to understand Scripture in a whole new light, in a way that I had not previously experienced. It all began to make sense. Furthermore, I began to greatly enjoy reading Scripture, treasuring His word in my heart.

---

[7] 1 Corinthians 1:18.

[8] There was a time that I sincerely wanted to understand and believe. I even convinced myself that I did in fact believe. However, reflecting on that time now, I realize that I was lying to myself. During that time, I found it a struggle to read Scripture as I thought it was boring and I did not seem to get anything out of it.

The words were the same words that they had always been, so what changed? It certainly had nothing to do with my intelligence or ability to comprehend. Rather, it was the Holy Spirit that enabled me to understand and embrace God's truth and love. Scripture explains this work of the Holy Spirit by stating:

> "For who knows the person's thoughts except the spirit of that person, which is in him? So also no one comprehends the thoughts of God except the Spirit of God. Now we have received not the spirit of the world, but the Spirit who is from God, that we might understand the things freely given us by God. And we impart this in words not taught by human wisdom but taught by the Spirit, interpreting spiritual truths to those who are spiritual. *The natural person does not accept the things of the Spirit of God, for they are folly to him, and he is not able to understand them because they are spiritually discerned.*"[9]

This passage explains that it is only through the power of the Holy Spirit that we are able to understand God's truth. Since no one is naturally born with the Holy Spirit, the "natural person" refers to someone who does not have the Holy Spirit dwelling within them and therefore is not able to understand God's truth. The ability to truly understand and embrace Scripture is not a matter of human intelligence. It is only by the Holy Spirit dwelling within you that enables Scripture to cause transformational growth.

To clarify, even with the Holy Spirit dwelling within us, we may have a hard time understanding different passages

---

[9] 1 Corinthians 2:11-14, emphasis mine.

of Scripture. It is perfectly normal to not understand all the wisdom and truth within Scripture, even as a Disciple of Christ with the Holy Spirit dwelling within you. Even Peter admits that some passages of Scripture are "hard to understand."[10] No Christian will understand everything in Scripture. We need to continuously pour ourselves into Scripture. With the Holy Spirit, we will continue to grow in our knowledge and understanding of God's word.

As we continue to spend time in God's word, we continue to grow in our relationship with Christ and grow in Christ. As we continue to grow in Christ, we continue to grow in our understanding of Scripture. This process continues through the rest of our earthly lives, like the rest of sanctification.

POWER OF GOD'S WORD

As we conform our life to the truths of Scripture, we will grow as image bearers of Christ. Christ lived a life in perfect obedience to God's commands. As Disciples of Christ, we should seek to follow His example. Yet, Jesus did not obey God's commands out of reluctance or out of a resentful obligation. Rather, He obeyed to demonstrate His trust in the Father, to glorify the Father, and out of His love for the Father. Our attitude in obeying God should follow Christ's example as well.

To follow Christ in obedience and in our attitudes will take a work of transformation. As Disciples of Christ, we have already experienced transformation through the work of the Holy Spirit; however, God uses Scripture as a tool to nurture and grow this transformation.

---

[10] 2 Peter 3:15-16 states, "And count the patience of our Lord as salvation, just as our beloved brother Paul also wrote to you according to the wisdom given him, as he does in all his letters when he speaks in them of these matters. There are some things in them that are hard to understand, which the ignorant and unstable twist to their own destruction, as they do the other Scriptures."

Near the end of His earthly ministry, Jesus prayed to the Father, asking the Father to bless, protect, and equip His disciples. In the middle of this prayer, Jesus prayed that the Father would "sanctify them in the truth; Your word is truth."[11] Sanctify means to make holy; it is a word that describes a transformation. In this passage, Jesus is praying that the Father would transform His disciples to reflect His holiness. The tool that Jesus asks God to use is "the truth." He then elaborates by saying, "Your word is truth." Jesus is asking the Father to transform us through the word of God; therefore, Scripture is one of the primary tools that causes us to grow to be more like Christ.

God puts power behind his words. It is by His words that creation came to exist. It is by hearing His word that we are called to faith in Christ. Paul wrote to the church of Rome, "so faith comes from hearing, and hearing through the word of Christ."[12] As we hear and reflect on God's word, God uses His word to renew our mind and cause transformation to our heart. Later in this same letter, Paul instructs the church to "not be conformed to this world, but be transformed by the renewal of your mind."[13] There is transformational power in God's word that causes us to grow. It is God's word that created us, brought us into salvation, and continues to transform us.

The author of Psalm 119 understood the power of God's word. As he meditated on God's word, he wrote the longest Psalm in Scripture. Psalm 119:11 states, "I have stored up your word in my heart, that I might not sin against You." Notice that the Psalmist states that he stored God's word in his heart. What does it mean to store something in our heart? We use a similar phrase in our day-and-age when we explain that we know something "by heart." To know something "by heart" means to have memorized it, which conveys the idea

---

[11] John 17:17.
[12] Romans 10:17.
[13] Romans 12:2.

that you have treasured the information so much that it lives in you.

The psalmist then explains that the purpose that he stored God's word in his heart was so that he would "not sin against" God. In order to store God's word in our heart, we have to know God's word. The more we study God's word, the more we are aware of sin and of God's righteousness. The more we read, study and know God's word, the more we come to know God and thus our relationship with God grows stronger. Furthermore, if we store God's word in our heart, then the word of God is in the exact location it needs to be to transform our heart. This transformation of the heart will then affect how we live our lives. The more we study and store God's word in our heart, the more we will be transformed to be like Christ; the more we grow in Christ, the less we will fall to the temptations of sin.

In fact, Jesus used Scripture to overcome the temptations of the devil. Shortly after His baptism, Jesus went out to the wilderness and fasted for forty days. During this time, the devil approached Jesus and tempted Him three times. However, Jesus countered each of Satan's temptations with Scripture. The devil even tried to use and manipulate God's word to tempt Jesus, but Jesus had stored up Scripture in His heart and therefore was able to use Scripture to overcome temptation and rebuke Satan's misuse of God's word.

During this time of temptation, Satan tempted Jesus with food, telling Jesus to turn the rocks into bread. Jesus had been fasting for forty days and was hungry. Of course, eating is not a sin, nor is it a sin for Jesus to use His divine power; however, Jesus was led out by the Holy Spirit to the wilderness to fast. To break the fast at that time would have been an act of disobedience and would demonstrate a lack of trust in the Father to provide for Him. In response to this temptation, Jesus quoted from Deuteronomy, stating, "It is written, 'Man shall not live by bread alone, but by every word that comes from the mouth of God.'"[14] Jesus told the devil that while food is good for nurturing the body, Scripture is better as it feeds the soul.

Satan tempted Jesus three times and each time Jesus used Scripture to fight back against the devil's attacks. Scripture is our sword to fight against spiritual warfare and our weapon to fight against temptation.[15] When we have Scripture stored in our heart (memorized) we will always be armed and ready to fight off temptation. The more Scripture we have memorized, the more we will be equipped to handle different situations. Therefore, I encourage all Disciples of Christ to not just simply read the Bible. Rather we receive more nutrients from Scripture when we also hear God's word preached, study His truth, memorize passages, and pray through Scripture. When we read, hear, study, memorize, and pray through Scripture we will receive more nutrients from God's words, which nurtures our growth in Christ.

However, reading, studying, and memorizing God's word should not be an academic practice. Knowing Scripture is not just about knowledge for the sake of knowledge; rather it should be thought of as a relational endeavor. When we spend time in God's word, God reveals Himself to us and we get to know God more from His own words. As we spend time in God's word, we are spending focused time with God Himself and the result of which is that we will grow in our relationship with Him.

DAILY SCRIPTURE READING

Being a Disciple of Christ is primarily about glorifying God and having a relationship with God. Therefore, it should be no surprise that Scripture reading should be an integral

---

[14] Matthew 4:4 quoting Deuteronomy 8:3.
[15] Ephesians 6:17 states, "and take the helmet of salvation, and the sword of the Spirit, which is the word of God."

part of our daily Christian life. Daily Scripture reading is an essential source of nutrients for our spiritual growth in Christ.

Consider the opening words of Psalm 1:

> "Blessed is the man who walks not in the counsel of the wicked, nor stands in the way of sinners, nor sits in the seat of scoffers; but his delight is in the law of the LORD, and on His law he mediates day and night. He is like a tree planted by streams of water that yields its fruit in its season, and its leaf does not wither. In all he does, he prospers."[16]

In this passage, the psalmist describes the "blessed man" whose "delight is in the law of the LORD." This is describing a person who loves God's word because He loves God. Since he recognizes that the words of God are for our good, the psalmist spends each day and night meditating on Scripture.

The Psalmist goes on to explain that this man is like a "tree planted by streams of water." Just as a stream of water provides essential nutrients to a tree, God's word pours into our soul, providing essential nutrients for our spiritual growth. Lastly, the Psalmist describes that this tree yields fruit due to the nutrients that it receives from the streams. Here the Psalmist is describing how it is through meditating on God's word that we are able to grow and bear fruit as a Disciple of Christ.

As you spend time reading, studying, meditating, and memorizing Scripture, I encourage you to apply the Listen, Learn, Live approach.[17] I have personally found this method to be extremely helpful in seeing the Word of God as more

---

[16] Psalm 1:1-3.

[17] I was taught the Listen, Learn, Live approach by Pastor Bubba Jennings at Resurrection Church, Tacoma, Washington.

than just words on a page. This model helps me not only understand Scripture, but also nurtures my spiritual growth.

LISTEN: When you first read a passage or chapter of Scripture, approach the text as someone listening to someone speak. The key question to ask yourself is: **What does this passage say?** To help answer this question, take time to write out a summary or outline the passage. As you read, note repeated words, phrases, and themes. Lastly, write down any questions that you have about the passage. Pray through those questions and re-examine the passage. The goal is simply to understand what the passage is about.

LEARN: After spending time listening to the passage, you will go a little deeper by seeking to understand the point of the text. The key question to ask yourself is: **What does this passage mean?** What is the point of the passage? Interview the text by asking Who, What, When, Where, and Why type questions. What does this passage reveal to us about God? What does the passage teach about what God has done, is doing, and will do? What does the passage teach about human nature? God's character?

As we dig into the word to understand a deeper meaning, we must remember that the words of Scripture are God's very words. Since God cannot error, then we can trust that Scripture is without error and cannot contradict itself. Therefore, we should use Scripture to understand Scripture.

If we have questions about a passage, we should search for answers by using other passages, starting with the verses that surround the passage in question. We always want to understand Scripture in context with the surrounding passages, in context with the rest of the chapter, the rest of the book, and the rest of the Bible. Ask yourself: Does this passage relate to other passages in the Bible? Do other passages of the Bible relate to this passage?

LIVE: After spending time reflecting and meditating on what a passage means, we should then begin living out God's word. The key question to ask yourself is: **How can I apply the truths of this passage in my life?** Is there a truth that should influence what you believe, how you feel, or how you behave? Is there a command to obey? Is there a sin to avoid? Is there an example to follow or avoid? Is there a promise to cling to?

Once you have identified the ways that the passage can be applied in your life, you will then need to conduct an alignment check on your heart. Do you embrace the truths taught in this passage in your mind, heart, and life? Are there areas in your life where you are not submitting to the truth revealed in the passage? If so, what is causing you to stumble (what idols are you clinging to)? How is God using this passage to transform you into His righteousness?

Lastly, ask yourself, how can you bless others with what is taught in this passage? As we live out the truths taught in Scripture, we should remember that God has saved us into community, therefore we should share what we have learned with others.

Admittedly, reading the Bible can initially seem daunting or even intimidating. These feelings can develop due to either the size of the Bible, the scope of the Bible, or even the majestic nature of the Bible. After all, these are God's very words. Regardless of what may cause these feelings, we must overcome them.

While knowing that these words are from God Himself may add to the daunting/intimidating factor, we must remember that God breathed out Scripture for us. It is through Scripture that God reveals Himself to us that we may better know Him. Do not worry about the size, scope, or even the majestic nature of the Bible. Rather, focus on your relationship with God, focus on God's love for you, and your love for God to drive you to His Word. If you struggle with the discipline of daily Scripture reading, then I encourage you to consider the following:

1) NECESSITY. Recognize that reading Scripture is a necessity for your spiritual growth, just as food is a necessity to your physical growth. Without it, you will become spiritually fatigued.

2) DEDICATE TIME. Make it a priority. Designate a set time to spend one on one time with God in His Word and in prayer. It is important to have a set time, because if you go with the attitude that you will do it when you find time, then you will likely never do it (there will always be other things competing to use your time). Being consistent in what time of day you read will help establish this discipline. Whether you read in the morning, during lunch, or evening, make it a regular discipline each day.

3) DAILY. When you first begin training yourself to read daily, do not get frustrated on how much (or little) you read. At this point it is more about getting into the word each day to spend time with God. In the beginning, try reading one chapter a day each day. Quality over quantity is the key during your daily time in the word. Don't try to rush through it to try to meet some quota. Seek what God is telling you in the chapter and meditate on how you can apply the message in your daily life.

4) GUARD YOUR HEART. Guard your heart from becoming legalistic in this discipline. Reading Scripture should never be about checking it off your list of daily things to do. To be clear, having a reading plan or even a checklist can be a useful tool to help keep you disciplined in your daily reading. However, as we implement these tools, we need to be aware that legalism lurks around the corner. Read with an open heart to be changed by God and to bring Him glory.

5) PRAY. Before you read, I encourage you to pray to God and ask the Holy Spirit to grant you focus, understanding, and to have your mind and heart transformed as you read. Prayer will greatly help prevent legalism and help prevent taking passages out of context.

6) VERSE BY VERSE. It is generally not helpful to randomly hop from one verse of one book to another verse in a different book. Rather, when you start a book, start at chapter one and continue through each chapter until you finish the book.[18] This will give you a better understanding of the overall theme or point of the book itself, which in turn will help you understand the verses that are contained within the book. This will help prevent you from taking a verse out of context.

7) FOR THE GLORY OF GOD. Above all, remember that we are not just reading to know more about God and we are not reading to improve our lives; we are reading to glorify God and to grow in relationship with Him. Let this be the heart-motivation that drives you to the word of God.

---

[18] See Appendix B for recommended reading plans. There are some reading plans that may have you hop to different books of the Bible, such as the Chronological Reading Plan. In these reading plans jumping from one book to another is by design to help build context.

Chapter 8
Grow In Christ: The Pillar of Prayer

COMMUNICATING WITH GOD

Prayer is the primary way in which we communicate with God. Communication is essential for a growing relationship. Therefore, prayer should be an important part of a disciple's life.

During His earthly ministry, Jesus would frequently turn to God the Father in prayer. Prior to calling His twelve disciples, Scripture records that "He went out to the mountain to pray, and all night He continued in prayer to God."[1] After Jesus miraculously fed five thousand people with five loaves of bread and two fish, He dismissed His disciples and the crowds, "and after He had taken leave of them, He went up on the mountain to pray."[2] On the night of His betrayal, Jesus went to the Garden of Gethsemane to pray, knowing that He was about to be crucified.[3] While being crucified, Jesus prayed, "Father, forgive them, for they know not what they do."[4] Clearly, spending time with God the Father in prayer was important to Jesus. Therefore, as a Disciple of Christ, we should follow His example.

Scripture teaches us to "rejoice always, pray without ceasing, give thanks in all circumstances; for this is the will of God in Christ Jesus for you."[5] We see that Jesus frequently went to God the Father in prayer, but what does it mean to pray without ceasing? To clarify, Scripture is not

---

[1] Luke 6:12.
[2] Mark 6:46; cross reference with Matthew 14:22-23, Luke 9:14-18, and John 6:8-15.
[3] Matthew 26:36 states, "Then Jesus went with them to a place called Gethsemane, and He said to His disciples, "Sit here, while I go over there and pray."
[4] Luke 23:34.
[5] 1 Thessalonians 5:16-18.

81

calling us to live every moment with our heads bowed, eyes closed, and hands raised. Rather, it is calling us to remember that God is always here, we have an ongoing, everlasting connection with God. We can always be in prayer with God, even as we go about our daily life. Sometimes our prayer will be more active, as in spending deliberate time focused on prayer. Other times our prayers will be more passive, in the back of our minds while we are working, spending time with friends, or doing our daily tasks.

Let us not make the mistake of thinking of prayer as simply talking to God. Rather, it's more helpful to think of prayer as a conversation with God. Communication in a conversation goes both ways, where both people take turns speaking and listening. Imagine you called up someone you care about and said, "Hey, it's me. Work is going well. I could use help this weekend on the project. Oh and I need some medicine for this cough I've been having. Thanks for everything. Bye." Then you end the call before you give the person a chance to respond. Did that even sound like a conversation? Absolutely not, that sounded more like leaving a message. Yet, how often do we pray in this manner? We call up God, let Him know some stuff going on in our life, ask for some pressing needs, and then we end the call with a respectful "amen." But prayer is not about leaving God a message; it's about having a conversation WITH God.

While God primarily talks to us through His written word (Scripture), He also speaks into our hearts through prayer. To be clear, I'm not saying that you will hear an audible voice (though that is not beyond God's ability), but you can hear from God in your prayers. I encourage you to have moments of silence in your prayer and open yourself to what God is telling you. Therefore, prayer is not just a time to speak to God, but also a time to listen. That being said, the best way to hear from God is through Scripture. When we combine our prayers with Scripture reading, we set ourselves up to engage God in a two-way conversation.

HOW TO PRAY

Some may feel uncomfortable praying and may feel that they don't know how to pray. In fact, Jesus' own disciples weren't sure how to pray. One day after Jesus finished praying, the disciples approached Jesus saying, "Lord, teach us to pray."[6] In response, Jesus taught His disciples what is commonly referred to as the "Lord's prayer." I have found this to be an unhelpful and misleading title since Jesus was not actually praying; rather, He was teaching them how to pray. A better title would be "The Lord's Model of Prayer."

To be clear, there is no one way to pray; while Jesus offers us a model, it is simply a model. It is *a* way to pray, not *the* way to pray. In fact, many of Jesus' prayers do not follow this model. We must not become legalistic and overly rigged in the format of our prayers.

Prayer is ultimately a way to enjoy our relationship with God and thus how you approach God in prayer may vary. We don't need to worry about the verbiage we use in prayer. There aren't requirements of what we must say or what we must not say. Simply focus on your restored relationship through Christ and open your heart to God. There really isn't a wrong way to pray as long as we approach God reverently, as a child to a parent. That being said, models of prayer can help direct, frame, and guide our prayers. One such model uses the acronym A.C.T.S., which is largely based on Jesus' model that He taught His disciples.

Adoration
Confession
Thanksgiving
Supplication

---

[6] Luke 11:1 states, "Now Jesus was praying in a certain place, and when He finished, one of His disciples said to Him, 'Lord, teach us to pray, as John taught his disciples.'"

ADORATION: 'A' stands for adoration. Our prayers begin by addressing who we are praying to, namely God. As we approach God in prayer, we should remember that we are coming before the Lord Creator of all creation and therefore should come with reverence and love.

When we begin our prayers in adoration, we come to God recognizing the greatness of God. Doing so reminds us of the character and attributes of God, that He is all powerful, all knowing, all present, a God of love and a God of justice. Beginning our prayers in adoration focuses our attention on God and helps comfort us as we reflect on His glory since all things are in His control and there is no prayer too big for God to receive. When Jesus taught His disciples to pray, He instructed them to start their prayers in adoration by addressing God as a loving father and by recognizing God's glory stating, "Our Father in heaven, hallowed be your name. Your kingdom come, your will be done, on earth as it is in heaven."[7]

CONFESSION: 'C' stands for confession. As we reflect on the glory of our perfect God, we will be reminded that we are not perfect. As we reflect on the goodness of God, we will be reminded that we have sinned against our loving creator. As we reflect on the love of God, we will be reminded that we fall short. Therefore, this should bring us to confess our sins and seek forgiveness. David demonstrates this process as he writes Psalm 38 to glorify and worship God during a time of pain. Near the end of this psalm David states, "I confess my iniquity; I am sorry for my sin."[8] Confessing our sins to God is both humbling and freeing. As we surrender our sin to God we open ourselves to receive His mercy, comfort, and power to overcome our sins. John encourages us to be honest about our sin by stating, "if we confess our sins, He is faithful and just to forgive us our sins

---

[7] Matthew 6:9-10; cross reference with Luke 11:2.
[8] Psalm 38:18.

and to cleanse us from all unrighteousness."[9] Jesus' model of prayer taught His disciples to confess their sins in prayer by instructing them to say, "forgive us our sins, for we ourselves forgive everyone who is indebted to us."[10]

THANKSGIVING: 'T' stands for thanksgiving. As we confess our sins to God, asking God for forgiveness, we should remember that God has forgiven us through Christ. Jesus came to earth and died on the cross for all our sins (past, present, and future). As Disciples of Christ, our sins have been forgiven. When we remember the atonement of Christ, a spirit of gratitude will lead us into thanksgiving, causing us to thank God for the love He has for us.

Yet God has blessed us with more than our salvation, He has showered us with numerous blessings and continues to do so each day. As we reflect on these many blessings, we will become more grateful and our thankful heart will lead us to better reflect the love of God. While thanksgiving is not explicitly mentioned in Jesus' model of prayer, there is certainly an undertone of thanksgiving throughout the model. Furthermore, Scripture teaches us to "continue steadfastly in prayer, being watchful in it with thanksgiving."[11]

SUPPLICATION: 'S' stands for supplication.[12] Admittedly, supplication is not a common word in our modern-day vocabulary. The word simply means to petition or to request. While it is generally our requests that drive us to pray to begin with, the A.C.T.S. model teaches us to make our requests last. Some mistakenly only go to God in prayer when they need something; yet this misses the point of

---

[9] 1 John 1:9.
[10] Luke 11:4; cross reference with Matthew 6:12.
[11] Colossians 4:2; cross reference with Philippians 4:6 and 1 Thessalonians 5:16-18. Also, note that 23 different Psalms call us to offer God thanks/thanksgiving.
[12] **Supplication:** A request, asking for something.

prayer. Praying and reflecting on adoration, confession, and thanksgiving before supplication helps give us a spiritual alignment check. It reminds us that prayer is more about our relationship with God and not the requests that we desire from God.

Furthermore, after we have reflected on the glory of God (adoration), our sins (confession), and the grace, forgiveness, and blessings that God has given us (thanksgiving)… what more can we really ask? I don't mean to minimize the situations or problems that cause us to come to God. I'm simply saying that after focusing our attention on God and away from the issue that brought us to God, we sometimes gain a new perspective and realize that the issue is not as bad as we originally thought. When we recognize the greatness of God and the many blessings that God has already given us, we can embrace any future trials knowing that God is greater than our circumstances, and we can trust Him in every situation. God can use any event for His glory and He frequently nurtures our growth through times of hardship.[13] Scripture teaches us to:

> "Rejoice in our sufferings, knowing that suffering produces endurance, and endurance produces character, and character produces hope, and hope does not put us to shame, because God's love has been poured into our hearts through the Holy Spirit who has been given to us."[14]

While we should not only come to God when we need something, we should not make the opposite mistake of never asking God for anything. God wants us to come to Him in prayer. Scripture tells us, "do not be anxious about anything, but in everything by prayer and supplication with

---

[13] This topic is explored in more detail in Chapter 5.
[14] Romans 5:3-5; cross reference with Philippians 1:29-30 and James 1:2-3.

thanksgiving let your requests be made known to God."[15] In this passage, Scripture calls us to not worry but instead to go to God in prayer.

God wants us to bring all our concerns, desires, problems, and dreams to Him, no matter how great or small we may think it. Is it that God does not know our needs? God is all-knowing and all-present; He knows the depths of our mind and heart. He already knows our situations, needs, and desires. Why then does He call us to pray? God calls us to pray because He desires a real relationship with us! When we turn to God in prayer, we are embracing the relationship that we have with God. When we trust in God and in our relationship with Him, then we can be comforted in any situation. God is all-powerful and the Lord of all creation; therefore, no situation is greater than God. Thus, when you go to God in prayer, Scripture tells us that "the peace of God, which surpasses all understanding, will guard your hearts and your minds in Christ Jesus."[16]

In His model for prayer, Jesus taught His disciples to go to God for their needs by stating, "Give us this day our daily bread."[17] In this statement, Jesus is teaching His disciples to ask God for provision, such as food. Yet, this is really an example for us to ask God for all our needs.

Jesus gives another example of supplication in His model when He closes with "lead us not into temptation, but deliver us from evil."[18] In this statement, Jesus is teaching His disciples to pray for protection from spiritual warfare. In fact, in the book of Ephesians, Paul goes on in some detail about spiritual warfare and explains that as Disciples of

---

[15] Philippians 4:6. Additionally James 1:5 states, "If any of you lacks wisdom, let him ask God, who gives generously to all without reproach, and it will be given him."

[16] Philippians 4:7. Notice the verse ends with the phrase, "in Christ Jesus." This is using relational language, to be "in Christ" is to be in relationship with Christ and to be transformed by the relationship.

[17] Matthew 6:11; cross reference with Luke 11:3.

[18] Matthew 6:13; cross reference with Luke 11:4.

Christ we have been equipped with what he calls the "Armor of God."[19] Paul then concludes his instruction on spiritual warfare by encouraging Disciples of Christ to be "praying at all times in the Spirit, with all prayer and *supplication*. To that end, keep alert with all perseverance, making *supplication* for all the saints."[20] Just as Scripture is our primary offensive tool in the battles of spiritual warfare, prayer is one of our primary defensive tools.

While the A.C.T.S. model of prayer can be a useful tool, there is no better way to learn how to pray than to read the Psalms. The book of Psalms is a collection of 150 prayers and provides a great example of how to pray. If you want to learn how to go to God in adoration, confession, thanksgiving, and supplication, read the Psalms. Psalm 111 is a great example of prayerful adoration. Psalm 51 is a great example of prayerful confession. Psalm 100 is a great example of prayerful thanksgiving. Psalm 86 is a great example of prayerful supplication. The Psalms are real prayers written by real people. Furthermore, each psalm is also Scripture and thus breathed out by God. Therefore, each psalm is a prayer that God Himself authored.

THE HOLY SPIRIT EMPOWERS PRAYER

The Holy Spirit empowers our prayers to cause spiritual growth. Scripture tells us to pray "at all times *in the Spirit*, with all prayer and supplication."[21] What does it mean to pray "in the Spirit?" It means to allow the indwelling Spirit to drive our prayers. Yet, this is often easier said than done.

When we pray, we frequently get in our own way and try to force the words. We become overly aware of each word

---

[19] Paul's warning of Spiritual Warfare and description of the "Armor of God" is recorded in Ephesians 6:10-20.

[20] Ephesians 6:18, emphasis mine.

[21] Ephesians 6:18, emphasis mine.

we say. If we pray in a group, we may even attempt to use more pious sounding words. When we do any of the above it makes the experience of prayer uncomfortable, unnatural, and may dissuade us from going to God in prayer.

Rather than trying to force the words or try to use "religious" language, we are to surrender to the Holy Spirit and trust Him with the words that need to be spoken.

Have you ever prayed to God or felt the need to pray, but did not know what to say? Perhaps there was a time when you prayed and the words that you spoke didn't seem quite right. Experiencing either of these situations can be confusing or even unsettling, but we can be comforted to know that the Spirit is here to help. Scripture explains one of the Holy Spirit's roles in prayer by stating:

> "Likewise the Spirit helps us in our weakness. For we do not know what to pray for as we ought, but the Spirit Himself intercedes for us with groanings too deep for words. And He who searches hearts knows what is the mind of the Spirit, because the Spirit intercedes for the saints according to the will of God."[22]

The Spirit helps us by praying to the Father on our behalf. We can rest assured that the Holy Spirit knows our prayers, He knows what we need to pray for better than we do ourselves. It is comforting to know that even when we go to God in prayer with nothing to say, the Spirit is praying on our behalf. Remember, prayer is not really about the words. It's about spending time with our loving God and enjoying the relationship that He gave us through His death.

While God knows our prayers through His omniscience, He also knows our prayers in a deeply personal way through

---

[22] Romans 8:26-27.

the Holy Spirit dwelling in us. Do you see God's love and desire for a personal relationship in this? His omniscience is perfectly sufficient to know our prayers, after all He knows our prayers before we even come to Him in prayer. Yet, since God desires to have a personal relationship with us, He gave us His Spirit to know our prayers in a more personal way.

With the assurance of the Holy Spirit praying on our behalf, we can turn to God in prayer for the sake of the relationship. We don't need to worry about what exactly needs to be said or about every little concern. We can trust that God already knows the details and therefore we can simply enjoy the relationship we have with God. When we pray in the Spirit our prayers become more focused on enjoying this relationship rather than the exact words. Yielding to the Spirit will change our prayers from obligatory words to a conversation with our loving Father.

Chapter 9
Grow In Christ: The Pillar of Fellowship

SAVED INTO RELATIONSHIP

As a Disciple of Christ, we have been saved into a relationship with God. The relationship between mankind and God is in a vertical sense as we look up to God and His glory. We relate to God in submission to His glory: God is our King; we are His servants. God is our Creator; we are His creation. God is our Father; we are His children. Scripture refers to our restored relationship as being adopted into God's family, stating that God has "predestined us for adoption to Himself as sons through Jesus Christ, according to the purpose of His will."[1] God is the head of the family and it is by His grace that we have been adopted as members into His family.

Since all Disciples of Christ are adopted into God's family, then that means that we are all adopted into the same family together! Therefore, the cross of Christ not only restored our relationship with God, but it also brought all disciples into relationship with each other. The relationship

---

[1] Ephesians 1:5; cross reference with Galatians 4:4-7 and Romans 8:14-25.

amongst disciples is in a horizontal sense, as we come together as brothers and sisters, side-by-side, to glorify God. We relate to each other in fellowship with one another.

Therefore, Disciples of Christ are saved into a relationship with God and with other believers. When we combine the respective shapes of these two relationships (the vertical relationship we have with God and the horizontal relationship we have with each other), we see that the restored relationships that we have through Christ forms the image of the cross. Thus, the cross is both the literal instrument that Christ used to restore our relationship and the figurative image of our restored relationship.

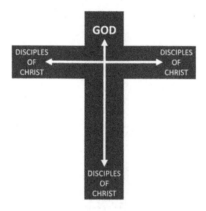

When Disciples of Christ come together in fellowship, we are coming together as a family. Since all believers are united by Christ, we can all band together to celebrate that we have been forgiven, cleansed of our sins, clothed in Christ's righteousness, and given a new shared identity in Christ. There is no greater reason to unite than under the banner of God's grace and glory.

As Disciples of Christ, we can have different ethnicities, come from different nations, different cultures, different walks of life, and we can share no common interests nor hobbies. Yet we can still come together in fellowship by the mere fact that we are members of the same family. Despite any differences we may have with each other, we can unite in the fact that we serve the one true God and we each share a common identity in Him. There is no other common denominator needed to unite other than embracing His divine truth and love. Therefore, Scripture tells us to "welcome one another as Christ has welcomed you, for the glory of God."[2]

THE HOLY SPIRIT EMPOWERS FELLOWSHIP

Just as the Holy Spirit empowers Scripture and prayer to cause spiritual growth, He also empowers our fellowship. Despite any cultural, political or economic differences that we may have with each other, we are all united in Christ. We are united in God's truth, in God's love, and in our identity that we have in Him. The Holy Spirit serves as a reminder and the glue of this unity. Scripture calls us to "maintain the unity of the Spirit in the bond of peace. There is one body and one Spirit – just as you were called to the one hope that belongs to your call – one Lord, one faith, one baptism, one God and Father of all, who is over all and through all and in all."[3]

As a Disciple of Christ, the same Holy Spirit who lives in me also lives in you and all other disciples. We are united, brought together as one. Furthermore, the indwelling Holy Spirit points to our adoption into God's family, as Scripture states:

---

[2] Romans 15:7.
[3] Ephesians 4:3-6.

93

"For all who are led by the Spirit of God are
sons of God. For you did not receive the spirit
of slavery to fall back into fear, but you have
received the Spirit of adoption as sons, by
whom we cry, 'Abba! Father!' The Spirit
Himself bears witness with our spirit that we
are children of God."[4]

Through the indwelling Spirit of God, we know that we
have been brought into God's family and thus enjoy a
genuine relationship with God.

To clarify, while it is through Christ that we are brought
into this family, it is by the power of the Holy Spirit that
connects us and sustains our relationship with God and with
each other. Yet, not only does the Holy Spirit connect us and
remind us of our unity, but He also empowers us to live as
united brothers and sisters.

If left to our own sinful nature, we would seek to only
serve ourselves. Scripture reveals that our sinful nature
produces "sexual immorality, impurity, sensuality, idolatry,
sorcery, enmity, strife, jealousy, fits of anger, rivalries,
dissensions, divisions, envy, drunkenness, orgies and things
like these."[5] Notice the fruits of our sinful nature are all
about our own self-interest and division. These fruits do not
build relationships, they destroy them, yet we are all born
with this nature of the flesh.

However, as Disciples of Christ, we have been given the
Spirit of God to dwell in us to transform our hearts. Scripture
explains that "the fruit of the Spirit is love, joy, peace,
patience, kindness, goodness, faithfulness, gentleness, self-
control."[6]

Where does this fruit come from? It comes from the Holy
Spirit. Notice that Scripture refers to these attributes as "the

---

[4] Romans 8:14-16.
[5] Galatians 5:19-21.
[6] Galatians 5:22-23.

fruit of the Spirit," indicating that the attributes listed are the product of the indwelling Holy Spirit living in us. These qualities do not come from us in our natural state, they are not part of our nature. We can only truly demonstrate and experience these characteristics through the power of the Holy Spirit living in us. To clarify, since all people are made in God's image, all people can demonstrate a faded image of these qualities, but it is not the same as the attributes that we experience through the indwelling power of the Holy Spirit. The difference is that the true divine attributes are unconditional and eternal. As an example, it is by the power of the Holy Spirit that you can experience true peace, despite the chaos of the world.

Notice that the word "fruit" in this passage of Scripture is singular. There are not nine different fruits. Rather, there is only one fruit with nine different components. Just as an apple is one fruit, yet we can break down the apple into different parts (the skin, the stem, the flesh, the core, etc.), the fruit of the Spirit is one fruit with nine parts. Just as an apple tree does not produce parts of an apple, the Spirit does not produce only parts of His fruit. We either have the fruit (and all its components) or we don't. I can't say that I have love and joy, but lack patience and self-control. It is all one fruit. If you have one aspect of it, you have it all.

The fruit of the Spirit are divine attributes and can only be experienced through God living in us. Therefore, if you struggle with being loving, joyful, at peace, patient, kind, good, faithful, gentle, or struggle with self-control, the answer is NOT to try harder and hope to do better. The answer is to submit to the power of the Holy Spirit dwelling within you. It is only through Him that we can truly experience and demonstrate these divine qualities.

Notice that the attributes created by the fruit of the Spirit can be used to encourage and strengthen our unity.[7] How amazing would our fellowship be if it were full of love, joy and peace? How much would we grow in our relationship if we showed each other patience, kindness, and goodness? Imagine what we could overcome as a family if we were gentle with each other, exercising self-control, and faithful to each other and to God. The fruit of the Spirit is essential for lasting unity.

THE IMAGE OF THE CHURCH

Fellowship completes the way we were made in the image of God. God, being a Triune being, is in eternal fellowship within Himself. Yet mankind is not a triune creature. It is only in our relationship with others that we can reflect God's image of eternal fellowship.

Fellowship is an essential aspect to our existence, which is proven by our desire to be in community with others and the mental breakdown that occurs when left in isolation for an extended period of time. God created us as social creatures. Shortly after creating Adam, God stated, "It is not good that the man should be alone," and then He created Eve.[8] We are meant to exist in fellowship with each other, similar to how God exists in eternal fellowship.

As Disciples of Christ, we are called to come together in united fellowship as a family. We refer to this family as the church. In our modern language, the word "church" is often

---

[7] Also notice that the Spirit produces a fruit that contrasts with the flesh, which creates an internal conflict. As Disciples of Christ, we have two natures (one of the Spirit and the other of the Flesh) and they are at war within us, "for the desires of the flesh are against the Spirit, and the desires of the Spirit are against the flesh, for these are opposed to each other, to keep you from doing the things you want to do" (Galatians 5:17). The opposing natures of the Flesh and Spirit was addressed in Chapter 4.

[8] Genesis 2:18 states, "Then the LORD God said, 'It is not good that the man should be alone; I will make him a helper fit for him.'"

used to describe a place where we can fellowship, worship, and learn more about God. However, the Bible never actually uses the term "church" to refer to a location or building. Rather, Scripture refers to the church as a group of people who are united in Christ. The church is not made of brick, wood, or steel, but of people who are united as one body in Christ. Just as a body is made of many parts that together form a body, the church is made of Disciples of Christ that together form the church.[9] Scripture goes on to say that Jesus "is the head of the body, the church."[10] Jesus is the high priest over the church, the head Shepherd who cares for the congregation, and the Lord who governs the church.

Not only are Disciples of Christ united in one body, but we each have a different purpose in the body. Scripture explains that "for as in one body we have many members, and the members do not all have the same function, so we, though many, are one body in Christ, and individually members one of another. Having gifts that differ according to the grace given to us, let us use them."[11] Just as our human body is one body, but made of different parts, each with their own purpose (eyes, ears, arms, legs, lungs, bones, etc.); likewise, each member of the church is made with their own gift to support the church body. Some are gifted to teach, others to sing, some are gifted to be compassionate and encouraging, while others are gifted to evangelize and so on. There are many different spiritual gifts that God has blessed different people. Therefore, we each have a role in the church body. Since every part is needed, we need each other to function as a church body. This means that each member of the church is called to give and serve the body. No member should be dormant.

---

[9] 1 Corinthians 12:27 states, "Now you are the body of Christ and individually members of it."
[10] Colossians 1:18.
[11] Romans 12:4-6.

Many have mistakenly approached church with a consumer mentality, expecting that their only role in church is to receive from the church leaders. This mentality puts all the work of ministry on the leader and can inspire unhealthy questions like, "what can this church do for me?" While it is true that the church leaders are called to lead and feed those in his congregation, the primary role of the local church leader is to "equip the saints for the work of ministry, for building up the body of Christ, until we all attain to the unity of faith and of the knowledge of the Son of God, to mature manhood, to the measure of the stature of the fullness of Christ."[12] The role of the local church leader is to help the members of the body grow in Christ and "equip" the congregation, which will enable the body "for the work of ministry." Therefore, the church member should not ask, "how can the church serve me?" Instead, members of a local church body should ask, "how can I serve in the church?"

Overall, the church is about deep, personal, genuine relationship with God and with fellow Disciples of Christ. As we come together and grow in maturity as a church body, we will grow in relationship with each other and in our relationship with God. The church is about unity and fellowship with other believers for the purpose of worshipping God, learning and teaching the truths of God, spreading the Good News across the world, and ultimately to glorify God.

Scripture describes a great example of this fellowship, stating:

> "They devoted themselves to the apostles' teaching and the fellowship, to the breaking of bread and the prayers. And awe came upon every soul, and many wonders and signs were

---

[12] Ephesians 4:12-13.

being done through the apostles. And all who believed were together and had all things in common. And they were selling their possessions and belongings and distributing the proceeds to all, as any had need. And day by day, attending the temple together and breaking bread in their homes, they received their food with glad and generous hearts, praising God and having favor with all the people. And the Lord added to their number day by day those who were being saved."[13]

We should follow the example established by the early church by coming together in fellowship to study God's word, partake in communion, pray, and support each other as a family.

FELLOWSHIP & SCRIPTURE: The disciples of the early church dedicated themselves to study "the apostles' teaching" in fellowship. We can follow this example when we come together to hear, read, and study Scripture. This happens when we attend a church service to hear a sermon or when we come together to study the bible as a small group.

While there is great benefit in reading and studying Scripture privately (as we enjoy a personal relationship with God), we should also read and study Scripture in a group setting. When we read privately, we can take time to spend meaningful time with God and meditate on His word as we study Scripture. When we read and study as a group, we can share our insights and learn from what others have learned in their studies. Also, reading Scripture as a group will provide opportunities to ask questions and explore passages that may be difficult to understand. Lastly, reading Scripture

---

[13] Acts 2:42-47.

as a group will help safeguard us from taking a passage out of context, misunderstanding Scripture, or misusing Scripture. Satan and his demons like to misuse and twist Scripture and will tempt us with a false understanding or false application.[14] Studying Scripture as a united church body will help protect us from these lies. While it can be painful to receive correction when we misunderstand or misuse God's word, it is a great opportunity to grow.

FELLOWSHIP & COMMUNION: The disciples of the early church came together to partake in communion, or as Acts 2:42 states, "to the breaking of bread." Communion is when Disciples of Christ come together in remembrance of Christ's sacrificial atonement by taking bread and wine. This practice was ordained by Christ on the night before He was crucified. It was the last meal Jesus would eat before being put to death, thus this practice is commonly referred to as the Last Supper. Scripture describes the event stating:

> "And when the hour came, He reclined at table, and the apostles with Him. And He said to them, 'I have earnestly desired to eat this Passover with you before I suffer. For I tell you I will not eat it until it is fulfilled in the kingdom of God.' And He took a cup, and when He had given thanks He said, 'Take this, and divide it among yourselves. For I tell you that from now on I will not drink of the fruit of the vine until the kingdom of God comes.' And He took bread, and when He had given thanks, He broke it and gave it to them, saying, 'this is my body, which is given for you. Do this in remembrance of me.' And likewise the cup after they had eaten, saying,

---

[14] Genesis 3:1-5 and Matthew 4:5-6 are two examples in Scripture where Satan misused God's word.

'this cup that is poured out for you is the new covenant in my blood.'"[15]

Similar to baptism, communion is a practice ordained by Christ Himself and therefore is an important part of Christian worship. Also, like baptism, communion is full of symbolic meaning. Communion has a strong connection with the Passover celebration since Jesus and His disciples were gathering to partake in the annual Passover meal when He first ordained the practice. Therefore, to understand the importance of communion, we first need to have a baseline understanding of Passover.

While still slaves in Egypt, God commanded the Israelites to make unleavened bread as they were about to depart from Egypt. He then commanded that they sacrifice a lamb and place its blood on their door posts. That night, God sent an angel of death against Egypt, but it passed over every door with the blood of a lamb. After this event, Pharaoh finally relented and let Israel go. From that time on God commanded the Israelites to celebrate Passover every year to remember and honor God's salvation from slavery.

Communion is not only connected to Passover due to first being administered during the Passover meal, but also both observances serve as a remembrance of God's salvation. Where Passover celebrates the salvation of God's people from slavery in Egypt, communion celebrates the salvation of God's people from slavery to sin. We do not sacrifice a lamb in communion because Jesus is the Lamb of God. He willingly sacrificed Himself as the ultimate Passover sacrifice so that God would pass over our sins and no longer count our transgression against us. Therefore, when we take the bread, we remember that Christ sacrificed His body to save us. When we take the wine, we remember that our sins have been atoned for by the blood shed by

---

[15] Luke 22:14-20; cross reference with Matthew 26:26-30 and Mark 14:22-25.

Christ. Furthermore, just as the Israelites celebrated Passover as a nation, Disciples of Christ are to celebrate communion as a church body to remember God's atoning sacrifice.

Communion represents our restored relationship with God and with other Disciples of Christ. Notice that the word communion has the same root as the word "community." The word is to communicate the idea of being united for a common purpose. The act of coming together to break bread and have a meal is a relational activity. As we take the bread and wine in remembrance of Jesus' atoning sacrifice, we should also remember that Jesus died for our sins to restore our relationship with God. Therefore, communion is not just a remembrance of Christ's sacrificial death, but also a symbol of our restored relationship with God and our fellowship with each other.

Furthermore, communion also looks forward to the fellowship we will have with Christ in the heavenly banquet. In fact, Jesus refers to this banquet shortly after the Passover meal by stating, "I assign to you, as my Father assigned to me, a kingdom, that you may eat and drink at my table in my kingdom and sit on thrones judging the twelve tribes of Israel."[16] Therefore, communion represents our salvation that we have in Christ, and it represents the purpose of our salvation, which is our restored relationship with God.

FELLOWSHIP & PRAYER: The disciples of the early church also came together in prayer. While there is great benefit in praying to God privately (as we enjoy a personal relationship with God), there is also great benefit in praying as a church body in community with each other.[17] When

---

[16] Luke 22:29-30; in addition to this verse, Jesus refers to the kingdom of heaven by using a banquet metaphor throughout His parables.
Cross reference Luke 14:15-24 with Matthew 22:1-14.

[17] This echoes the same points made in the "Fellowship & Scripture" section. Just as there is a benefit to reading Scripture privately and in a group setting, there is a benefit to praying privately and as a group for similar reasons.

Disciples of Christ come together in prayer, they become united in their fellowship with God. This united effort fosters relational growth amongst each other and fosters a relational growth toward God as a church body.

Furthermore, praying in front others is an intimate act where we share our relationship with God with others. On the same note, when we hear others pray, we are being invited into their relationship with God. Communal prayer is an act in which Disciples of Christ open up to bare the troubles of their soul and the praises of the heart to both God and fellow Disciples of Christ. It is an act where we allow ourselves to be vulnerable in front of our brothers and sisters in Christ, which demonstrates a level of trust.

Lastly, hearing others pray over us and praying over others as a church community can be encouraging and fosters trust. The more we grow to trust each other, the more we grow in relationship with each other and the more we grow in relationship with God as a church body.

FELLOWSHIP & SUPPORT: As we continue to examine the example of fellowship set by the early church, we see that they supported each other by "selling their possessions and belongings and distributing the proceeds to all, as any had need."[18] This is a great example for us to follow, we should all be ready and willing to sacrificially give to help those in need. While this passage comments on how Disciples of Christ came together to support each other with material needs, we can extend this concept to include intangible needs as well. In addition to giving wealth, we can give our time, and use our spiritual gifts in the service of the church body.

Scripture tells us to "encourage one another and build one another up."[19] As we build each other up, we are helping each other grow in Christ. There will be times when we

---

[18] Acts 2:45.
[19] 1 Thessalonians 5:11.

struggle and fall to our temptations. In these times, the church body can come together to help each other in our struggles, remembering that we are each on the same journey of sanctification. Therefore, we should not scold or shun those who are struggling with their sins. Instead, we should help each other in our personal battles in a united effort. There will be times that life gets tough and the weight of it all is overbearing. While we ultimately have our rest in Christ, Scripture also tells us to "bear one another's burdens, and so fulfill the law of Christ."[20] Overall, as a church body we are called to care for each other, help each other grow, support each other in times of need, and ultimately love each other in a way that glorifies God.

THE IMPORTANCE OF FELLOWSHIP

An important part of fellowship as a Disciple of Christ is discipleship. Discipleship is when we invest into each other's lives to help each other grow in Christ, as the proverb says, "Iron sharpens iron, and one man sharpens another."[21] We are called to "sharpen" each other so that we can be better today than we were yesterday.

But how does iron sharpen iron? It takes friction from one piece of iron to remove bits of iron from the other (and thus it is sharpened). In the moment, it generally doesn't feel good when you are the one being sharpened. We don't like to have friction in our relationships, so we avoid it. Having bits of you being removed is not pleasant. This unpleasantness will make us want to avoid being corrected or lash out in a defiant defense. We must resist the "fight or flight" impulse and embrace the correction, knowing that it

---

[20] Galatians 6:2. Similarly Romans 15:1-2 states, "we who are strong have an obligation to bear with the failings of the weak, and not to please ourselves. Let each of us please his neighbor for his good, to build him up."
[21] Proverbs 27:17.

is for our good. "Whoever loves discipline loves knowledge, but he who hates reproof is stupid."[22]

Yes, friction is uncomfortable, yet the product of this friction is being sharpened. Just as an iron knife is more effective when it is sharpened, we are more effective in our calling when we are "sharpened."

We see an example of this correction take place in the book of Acts when a man named Apollos began preaching in Ephesus. Scripture states that Apollos was "competent in the Scriptures" and "he spoke and taught accurately the things concerning Jesus, though he knew only the baptism of John."[23] Apollos knew the Old Testament well and was able to connect its teachings to Jesus; yet, his understanding about Jesus and the gospel was lacking as He only knew about His baptism. After hearing Apollos teach, fellow Disciples of Christ named Priscilla and Aquila "took him aside and explained to him the way of God more accurately."[24]

How does Apollos respond to this correction? Does he run away or get defensive? Apollos responded by embracing the correction and learned from his fellow brother and sister in Christ. Equipped with this correction, Apollos went on to be a predominant leader in the church of Corinth in whom Paul considers to be a fellow servant of Christ.[25]

While receiving correction can be painful, we need to be careful in how we respond. The human impulse is to be defensive when we receive correction, regardless if we are right or wrong. While it may be painful, we should

---

[22] Proverbs 12:1.

[23] Acts 18:24-25 states, "Now a Jew named Apollos, a native of Alexandria, came to Ephesus. He was an eloquent man, competent in the Scriptures. He had been instructed in the way of the Lord. And being fervent in spirit, he spoke and taught accurately the things concerning Jesus, though he knew only the baptism of John."

[24] Acts 18:26.

[25] 1 Corinthians 3:5-6 states, "What then is Apollos? What is Paul? Servants through whom you believed, as the Lord assigned to each. I planted, Apollos watered, but God gave the growth." Cross reference with 1 Corinthians 4:6; 16:12 and Titus 3:13.

prayerfully consider the correction, no matter how painful it may be. As Scripture tells us, "for the moment all discipline seems painful rather than pleasant, but later it yields the peaceful fruit of righteousness to those who have been trained by it."[26]

We need each other to grow in Christ. Scripture stresses this importance by stating, "let us consider how to stir up one another to love and good works, not neglecting to meet together, as is the habit of some, but encouraging one another, and all the more as you see the Day drawing near."[27] Notice the emphasis this passages places on meeting regularly by stating, "not neglecting to meet together, as is the habit of some." We should be excited to come together as a family to encourage each other to love others, conduct good works, and to glorify God. None of us are going to do this perfectly, so we need each other to stir each other up and keep each other accountable to our identity in Christ.

---

[26] Hebrews 12:11.
[27] Hebrews 10:24-25.

Chapter 10
Grow In Christ: Foundational Love

Let us remember that the three pillars are built on the foundation of glorifying God. To clarify, the three pillars of growth are not the foundation, rather they are the essential framework that is built on the foundation.

As previously explored, we glorify God in our relationship with God. Therefore, glorifying God and enjoying our relationship with Him must be the reason that Disciples of Christ read Scripture, pray, and fellowship.[1] Notice that the three pillars of growth satisfy two of the three keys of a growing relationship: communication and time together. But what about the third key: love? Love is what keeps the whole thing together and points back to the foundation, because without love the whole building falls.

---

[1] This sentence echoes the Westminster Shorter Catechism's first question and answer: "What is the chief end of man? Man's chief end is to glorify God, and to enjoy Him forever."

Let us never forget that the only reason that we can enjoy a relationship with God is because of God's love for us, "for God so loved the world, that He gave His only Son, that whoever believes in Him should not perish but have eternal life."[2] In our sin, we rebelled against God, separated ourselves from Him, and condemned ourselves to death. Yet, even in our rebellion, God still loved us and offered us grace by taking on flesh to die for our sins.

Paul wrote on this matter to the church of Rome stating, "God shows His love for us in that while we were still sinners, Christ died for us."[3] Due to God's love for us, Jesus died on the cross to forgive us of our divine treason and to restore our relationship with Him. Scripture states:

> "For if while we were enemies we were reconciled to God by the death of His Son, much more, now that we are reconciled, shall we be saved by His life. More than that, we also rejoice in God through our Lord Jesus Christ, through whom we have now received reconciliation."[4]

Glory be to God, for He loved us when we were unlovable. Let us never forget that we are only able to love God because God loved us first.[5]

As Disciples of Christ, our response to God's love should be to love God above all things. When we love God above all things, we are glorifying Him above all things. Notice that love is again using relational language and indicates a genuine relationship with God. Therefore, loving God above all connects both to our relationship with God and giving

---

[2] John 3:16.
[3] Romans 5:8.
[4] Romans 5:10-11.
[5] 1 John 4:19 states, "We love because He first loved us."

glory to God. This understanding explains why Jesus says that the greatest command is to "love the Lord your God with all your heart and with all your strength and with all your mind."[6] In saying this, Jesus is saying that the greatest command is to love God with our whole being. This fulfills the purpose of our creation and the purpose of our salvation.

Just like any other strong relationship, love must be the foundational motivation for communication and spending time together. I can easily communicate and spend time with people in a way that is not loving, but if I don't love them then our relationship will not grow. Love is the underlying power that enables our communication and time together to cause relational growth. This is true for all relationships, to include our relationship with God. Therefore, we must ultimately read Scripture, pray, and fellowship out of our love for God.

Let us make sure we have our priorities straight. If our foundational reason to read Scripture is not about loving God, then we will become legalistic like the Pharisees. While we should value God's word more than gold and silver,[7] we should not make Scripture an idol. How foolish would it be to love someone's words more than the person who spoke them? Rather we should love a person's words because we love the person speaking the words. Yet, we find that our hearts are prone to fall in this trap. Jesus challenged this notion stating, "You search the Scriptures because you think that in them you have eternal life; and it is they that bear witness about me."[8] We should love Scripture *because* they are the very words of God Himself!

Through Scripture we come to know God's love for us. Every word He gives us is given out of His love for us. Furthermore, through Scripture we come to know God Himself. As Disciples of Christ, we do not study Scripture

---

[6] Matthew 22:37.
[7] Cross reference with Psalm 19:7-11; 119:72, 127; Proverb 16:16.
[8] John 5:39.

for the sake of knowledge or out of a legalistic obligation. Rather we read and study Scripture to glorify God motivated out of a desire to know Him better and therefore to grow in our relationship with Him.

If our foundational reason to pray is not about loving God, then our prayers will be empty words. When Jesus taught His disciples to pray, He told them, "And when you pray, do not heap up empty phrases as the Gentiles do, for they think that they will be heard for their many words. Do not be like them, for your Father knows what you need before you ask Him."[9] Furthermore, we do not want to make a show out of our prayer. Can you imagine being in a relationship with someone and the only time that this person talks to you is to show off their own greatness or intelligence? This would be self-worship and is a trap that our hearts can fall into if our prayers are not first and foremost motivated out of our love for God. Jesus rebuked this showmanship stating, "when you pray, you must not be like the hypocrites. For they love to stand and pray in the synagogues and at the street corners, that they may be seen by others. Truly, I say to you, they have received their reward."[10] As Disciples of Christ, we should not pray to try to manipulate God or to show off to others. We should pray to God out of our love for God and thus grow in our relationship.

If our foundational reason to fellowship is not about loving God, then we are committing idolatry by holding our worldly relationships above our relationship with God. While loving others is essential, it must be built upon the foundation of our love and glory to God. Notice that it is only *after* declaring that the greatest commandment is to love God, Jesus states, "a second is like it: You shall love your neighbor as yourself."[11] Jesus is saying that the second

---

[9] Matthew 6:7-8.
[10] Matthew 6:5.
[11] Matthew 22:39.

greatest commandment is to love others, second only to our love for God. Therefore, loving others is greatly important, it is indispensable, and it is a crucial part of a Disciple's life; it just cannot be above our love for God. We should love God first. We demonstrate God's love to others out of the abundance of love God has for us. Scripture tells us, "beloved, if God so loved us, we also ought to love one another."[12] As Disciples of Christ, we should fellowship to collectively spend time with God as adopted children brought into His family. Scripture calls us to, "love one another, for love is from God, and whoever loves has been born of God and knows God."[13] In fact, Jesus said, "by this all people will know that you are my disciples, if you have love for another."[14]

It is important to remember that we read Scripture, pray, and fellowship with each other out of our love for God. When the love of God drives us to study Scripture, pray, and fellowship as a family, we will "grow in the grace and knowledge of our Lord and Savior Jesus Christ. To Him be the glory both now and to the day of eternity. Amen."[15]

---

[12] 1 John 4:11.
[13] 1 John 4:7.
[14] John 13:35.
[15] 2 Peter 3:18.

G R O W	**"Rather, speaking the truth in love, we are to GROW up in every way into Him who is the head, into Christ."** **~Ephesians 4:15** • Are you growing in Christ? • Do you treat Scripture, prayer, and fellowship as essential in your life? Do you read Scripture daily? Do you pray daily? Do you regularly enjoy the fellowship with other believers? • Who causes spiritual growth to happen? What role does love have in our spiritual growth? What role does the Holy Spirit have?

*** PAUSE HERE TO PRAYFULLY REFLECT ON THE
ABOVE PASSAGE & QUESTIONS ***

PART III
GO FOR CHRIST

"**GO** therefore and make disciples of all nations, baptizing them in the name of the Father and of the Son and of the Holy Spirit, teaching them to observe all that I have commanded you. And behold, I am with you always, to the end of the age."
~ Matthew 28:19-20

Chapter 11
Go For Christ: Diplomatic Mission

AMBASSADORS OF CHRIST

The night before His crucifixion, Jesus prayed to God the Father for His disciples. In this prayer He asked the Father to watch over and bless His disciples after He had gone. It is a deeply personal prayer where Jesus appeals to the Father on our behalf, which is why it is often called "The High Priestly Prayer."[1] During this prayer, Jesus states:

> "I have given them your word, and the world has hated them because they are not of the world, just as I am not of the world. I do not ask that you take them out of the world, but that you keep them from the evil one. They are not of the world, just as I am not of the world... As you sent me into the world, so I have sent them into the world."[2]

Notice that in this prayer Jesus states that His disciples are not of the world, just as Jesus is not of the world. As Disciples of Christ, we have been made holy through the blood of Christ and are now separated from the fallen world. Therefore, as Disciples of Christ, we are in the world, but not of the world. Notice that Jesus specifically states that He isn't asking for His disciples to be taken out of the world. He

---

[1] This prayer is recorded in John 17. John 17 is a powerful passage that all Disciples of Christs should take the time to read, study, pray and mediate on, as these are words Jesus spoke shortly before His arrest and crucifixion. In John 17:20, Jesus states, "I do not ask for these only, but also for those who will believe in me through their word." Therefore, this prayer was not just for the disciples of the time, but all Disciples of Christ throughout time.
[2] John 17:14-16, 18.

sends us in the world that we may declare the good news of His truth and love.

As Disciples of Christ, we are called to proclaim the gospel and serve others. After Jesus' death and resurrection, Jesus charged His disciples to share the Good News of His redeeming work to others that they too may enjoy a restored relationship with God.

Shortly before Jesus ascended back to His heavenly throne, He explained to His disciples that they would receive power from the Holy Spirit to be His "witnesses in Jerusalem and in all Judea and Samaria, and to the end of the earth."[3] As Disciples of Christ, we are called to be His "witnesses." A witness is someone called to give their testimony, and thus we are called to share our testimony of Jesus' work and proclaim the truth that has been revealed to us. Jesus has empowered us to be his witnesses by sending the Holy Spirit to be our Helper and Comforter. With Christ now sitting on His throne, Disciples of Christ are called to be His representatives to the world.

We must remember that we have been adopted into God's family. In our adoption, we are no longer citizens of the fallen world as we are no longer of the world. Rather, we have been made citizens of His heavenly kingdom, as Scripture states "our citizenship is in heaven, and from it we await a Savior, the Lord Jesus Christ."[4] We belong to the kingdom of God and we have been sent to the world as representatives of that Kingdom to those who do not know Him. As Scripture states, "we are ambassadors for Christ, God making His appeal through us."[5] As ambassadors for Christ, God uses us to appeal to the world; therefore, our actions (both our words and deeds) should reflect Christ.

---

[3] Acts 1:8.
[4] Philippians 3:20.
[5] 2 Corinthians 5:20.

AMBASSADORIAL WORK

During Jesus' earthly ministry, Jesus served others and did not miss an opportunity to teach others about the Kingdom of God. As ambassadors of Christ, we should follow His example by giving and serving others.

While it is good that we serve, we must always remember that we are not doing these works for our own salvation, nor are we doing them to boast to others about our good deeds. Again, Scripture clearly states that we are not saved by our works, yet we were saved to do good works:

> "By grace you have been saved through faith. And this is not your own doing; it is the gift of God, not a result of works, so that no one may boast. For we are His workmanship, created in Christ Jesus for good works, which God prepared beforehand, that we should walk in them."[6]

These good works are a great way for Disciples of Christ to represent God as His ambassadors. In these works, we share the love of God with those who do not yet know Him and they can serve as a testimony to God's goodness. However, we should always remember that these works are done first and foremost to glorify God and are conducted to serve our diplomatic mission.

As we go out as ambassadors of Christ, we are called to share God's love with others by giving in four different areas. These are the four 'Ts' of giving:[7]

---

[6] Ephesians 2:8-10.

[7] The four 'T's' of giving was first taught to me by Pastor Bubba Jennings at Resurrection Church, Tacoma, WA. Mark Driscoll also refers to "giving" in terms of "treasures, talents, and time" (*Who Do You Think You Are?*, 132). As mentioned in chapter 9, we should also give in these areas as a way to serve the church body.

Time
Talent
Treasure
Testimony

TIME: In whatever way we may be called to serve or give, we will be called to give our time. The way we use our time is a strong indicator of what we love and value. Knowing this can be helpful for us to recognize the idols that we are tempted with and competing for God's place in our heart. Some consider their time as their most precious resource since we can never get back the time we spend.

Idolizing our time makes it difficult to give our time to others. Yet, as Disciples of Christ, we should be comforted in knowing that while our time on this earth is limited, we will live forever in eternity. Therefore, we should not covet our earthly time. On the other hand, we should realize that our time on this earth is limited and that is all the more reason that we should use this time wisely. Scripture teaches us that we should "walk in wisdom toward outsiders, making the best use of the time."[8] We must be mindful with how God calls us to spend our time and be ready to serve even when we feel that it's an inopportune time. There is no greater use of time than proclaiming the gospel to others, while we still have time to do so.

TALENT: God has given us spiritual gifts and talents to serve others as Scripture tells us:

> "As each has received a gift, use it to serve one another, as good stewards of God's varied grace: whoever speaks, as one who speaks oracles of God; whoever serves, as one who serves by the strength that God

---

[8] Colossians 4:5.

supplies – in order that in everything God may be glorified through Jesus Christ. To Him belong glory and dominion forever and ever. Amen."[9]

Remember, we are each a member of the church body. Just as our body is made of different parts with their own functions (we have eyes to see, ears to hear, etc.), each Disciple of Christ has their own function to support the body of Christ. We should not become boastful in our skills and talents since they are ultimately from God. These are gifts given to us to edify each other and to share God's love with those who do not yet know Christ.

Jesus set a great example for us by using His talents and abilities to serve others. Throughout His earthly ministry, Jesus would frequently use His gifts to help people in practical ways (such as healing the sick, curing the blind, casting out demons, etc.). He did not make a show of it. He used the opportunity to teach others about God's truth, justice, goodness, greatness, and love. He did not demand payment, but He simply helped people out of His love for them and to glorify God.

TREASURE: As Disciples of Christ, we are called to give our treasures, belongings, and money to serve others. Scripture states that "each one must give as he has decided in his heart, not reluctantly or under compulsion, for God loves a cheerful giver."[10] Disciples of Christ should not view financial/material giving as a burden, nor should it be done out of compulsion, nor out of reluctance, but out of faith, joy, and love.

Similar to giving our time, giving our money can be challenging for many as money is a common idol that the world worships. We often place our faith in wealth and find

---

[9] 1 Peter 4:10-11.
[10] 2 Corinthians 9:7.

security in what we own and have in savings. Or we feel insecure when we feel we do not have enough saved. These are symptoms that indicate that we are placing too much faith in our earthly treasures and not enough faith in God's provision. Also, similar to giving our time, how we spend our money can be a good indicator of what we love and value. Jesus warns us by stating:

> "Do not lay up for yourselves treasures on earth, where moth and rust destroy and where thieves break in and steal, but lay up for yourselves treasures in heaven, where neither moth nor rust destroys and where thieves do not break in and steal. For where your treasure is, there your heart will be also... ... No one can serve two masters, for either he will hate the one and love the other, or he will be devoted to the one and despise the other. You cannot serve God and money."[11]

To clarify, money is not evil, nor is it good. Money has no moral value in and of itself. It is how we view and use money that is often the problem. Some use their wealth for evil or do evil to gain money, for these people money is an idol that has replaced God. For others, they use their wealth to bless others, as they recognize that God has put them in a position to help others. The issue is not money; the issue is the human heart.

Jesus spoke much on financial giving and taught many parables to stress the point. During His sermon on the mount, Jesus taught that it is good to give to the needy. Yet, He warned that we should not make a show of it, nor should we boast about our giving. When we do so, then we are giving our treasure to be praised and for our glory, not the glory of

---

[11] Matthew 6:19-21, 24.

God. Rather, Jesus tells us that when we give to the needy, "do not let your left hand know what your right hand is doing, so that your giving may be in secret. And your Father who sees in secret will reward you."[12]

Once we are able to profess with our heart (instead of just our mouth) that God is the creator of the universe, then we will realize that everything in the universe is His. Everything that we have is only ours because God has given it to us (and in actuality, it still belongs to God). We acknowledge this fact and profess our faith in this fact by giving tithes and offerings to the church. We are also called to give our treasures to help those in need. We see great examples of giving in the early church where "all who believed were together and had all things in common. And they were selling their possessions and belongings and distributing the proceeds to all, as any had need."[13]

Financial giving is a way to serve our church, community, and other people. It is also an expression of genuine faith that God is the creator of everything, so we give back to Him to acknowledge that all belongs to Him. Lastly, it is a statement of faith and trust that God will provide.

TESTIMONY: The most important thing that Disciples of Christ are called to give is their testimony of Christ's love, truth, and gift of salvation. Giving our time, talents, and treasures should ultimately serve to provide an opportunity to proclaim Christ to others. There is no greater proclamation of love than the gospel; therefore, there is no greater act of service than to declare the gospel to those who do not yet know Christ.

At this point, it is helpful to make a distinction between sharing our testimony (being a witness of Christ) and proclaiming the gospel (evangelism). Sharing our testimony

---

[12] Matthew 6:3-4.
[13] Acts 2:44-45.

of Christ is simply to share what Christ has done in our life, sharing how having a restored relationship with God has impacted our life, and testifying our eye-witness account of God's greatness. Evangelism is specifically when we share the gospel, *the* Good News, which is the specific message that Jesus came and died on the cross to forgive us of our sins and restore our relationship with God. It is possible to share our testimony without sharing the gospel, and it is possible to share the gospel without sharing our testimony.[14] I bring up this distinction to serve as a reminder that just because someone shared their testimony does not necessarily mean that they shared the gospel. While there is a distinction between sharing our testimony and sharing the gospel, they do not have to be exclusive. In fact, sharing our testimony is much more beneficial when we also deliberately and explicitly proclaim the gospel. We do this when we explain how the gospel of Christ has impacted our life.

We must remember that a person's testimony in-and-of itself does not have the power to save anyone. Only the gospel has that power, as Scripture states that the gospel "is the power of God for salvation to everyone who believes."[15] Therefore, when we share our testimony of how Christ called us into His family and the impact that Jesus has had in our life, we should be mindful to declare the gospel. When we share our testimony, we should explain that it is through Christ's work on the cross that brought us into this relationship.

There is an old saying that says, "preach the gospel, use words if necessary." The point of this phrase is to highlight that our actions and lives should be a living testimony of the gospel. While this saying may have an appearance of wisdom, and even has some truth to it, it is a foolish phrase. It is equivalent to telling people to "feed the hungry, use food

---

[14] In fact, in the previous sentence I just shared the gospel without sharing my testimony.
[15] Romans 1:16.

if necessary."[16] Just as you cannot feed someone without food, you cannot preach the gospel without words.

While it is true that our lives should be a living testament to the gospel, we still must use words to proclaim the gospel. The word "gospel" literally means "Good News." News is communicated through words; therefore, you cannot share the gospel without using words. As good as our lives and our works may appear to the world, they will never communicate the gospel in and of themselves. While our works can be a beacon that points people to the gospel, if our good deeds are left without any proclamation of the gospel they will only point to self-righteousness.

It takes words to communicate that we are sinners doomed to damnation. It takes words to communicate that God, full of grace, sent Jesus to die on the cross to redeem us of sins and restore our relationship with God. It is only through words that we can communicate how the gospel has impacted our lives and transformed our identity. People will never know the gospel of Christ, until someone shares the message of the cross with them. As Scripture points out:

> "How then will they call on Him in whom they have not believed? And how are they to believe in Him of whom they have never heard? And how are they to hear without someone preaching? ... So faith comes from hearing, and hearing through the word of Christ."[17]

Our testimony of Christ's love serves to remind us of God's work in our life, which can be comforting during

---

[16] Ligon Duncan, "Saying, "Preach the Gospel, Use Words If Necessary" Is like Saying, "Feed the Hungry, Use Food If Necessary.","" Twitter (Twitter, October 31, 2017), last modified October 31, 2017, accessed January 1, 2021, https://twitter.com/ligonduncan/status/925541401554759680?lang=en.

[17] Romans 10:14, 17.

times of hardship and encouraging during times of prosperity. Furthermore, sharing how the gospel has impacted our life can be impactful to those who do not know Christ. Our testimony of God's love working in our life can be a seed of hope for others.

When we give our time, talent, and treasures, we should make it known that God's love enables our actions. He empowers us to be able to serve and whatever blessing we are able to provide is really from God Himself.

Chapter 12
Go For Christ: Proclaiming the Gospel

One of Jesus' last commands to His disciples was to "go into all the world and proclaim the gospel to the whole creation."[1] Clearly this command is important to Jesus, so let me ask you a question: what is the gospel?

Do not skip over this question. Stop reading and proclaim the gospel to yourself. If you were to share the gospel with someone, what would you say?

Many Disciples of Christ have a hard time expressing the gospel because they are not quite sure what to say. If you are someone who found themselves stumped by the question, not quite knowing how to answer it, know that you are not alone. This is something that we need to get better at, after all, Jesus specifically commanded us to proclaim the gospel. How can we be obedient to that command if we don't know what to say? As Peter stated, "honor Christ the Lord as holy, always being prepared to make a defense to anyone who asks you for a reason for the hope that is in you; yet do it with gentleness and respect."[2] We need to be prepared to explain the hope we have in Christ, every Disciple of Christ should be prepared to proclaim the gospel.

There are three important points to explain when proclaiming the gospel:

- Separation: The Need for the Gospel
- Christ: The Gospel Solution
- Relationship: The Purpose of the Gospel

---

[1] Mark 16:15.
[2] 1 Peter 3:15.

SEPARATION: THE NEED FOR THE GOSPEL

First, we need to address sin. This is uncomfortable and is what makes sharing the gospel offensive to hear. We are telling people that they have sinned and need help. Most people do not like hearing that they are wrong, nor do they like being called out on their mistakes. Many will not want to admit that they have done anything wrong. Yet, we know that "all have sinned and fall short of the glory of God."[3] Therefore, when we share the gospel, we are calling people to repent of their sins. As we explore this element, we should address two questions: What is sin, and what is the consequence of sin?

What is sin? Sin is to miss the mark of God's perfection; it is to fall short of God's glory. There are two primary ways we sin. We either do something that God has commanded us not to do, or we don't do something that God has commanded us to do.

1) Sin of Commission: When we do something that God has told us not to do, then we a committing an action that is against God's commands.[4] Eight of the Ten Commandments are things that we should not do: Do not have another god, do not worship idols, do not take the LORD's name in vain, do not murder, do not steal, do not commit adultery, do not lie, and do not envy. If you commit any of these actions, then you are committing a sin. To clarify, I am only using the Ten Commandments as an example, sins of commission are not limited to these eight commands. Any time we do anything that God has told us not to do, then we are committing a sin.

2) Sin of Omission: When we do not do something that God has commanded us to do, then we are sinning by omitting to fulfill God's commands.[5] James tells us that

---

[3] Romans 3:23.

[4] **Sin of Commission:** Committing an action that God has told us not to do.

[5] **Sin of Omission:** Omitting to do an action that God has commanded us to do.

"whoever knows the right thing to do and fails to do it, for him it is sin."[6] For example, Jesus commands us to make disciples and to proclaim the gospel to others. If you are ignoring this command, then you are omitting to do what God has commanded and thus you are sinning.

Therefore, we sin when we commit an action that we should not do, or when we omit an action that we should do. Have you ever done something that you weren't supposed to do? Have you ever neglected to do something that you knew you should have done? We all have, thus we have all sinned.

Ultimately, sin is to reject the commands of our Lord and Creator; it is to reject God. All sin is an act of rebellion against God. Sin is an act of cosmic treason against the King of the Universe, where we attempt to usurp God by placing something else in His place. When we sin, we are stating that we value something else more than we value God and His commands for us. Sin is to effectively worship something other than God, giving glory to something other than God.[7]

What is the consequence of sin? Scripture tells us that "the wages of sin is death."[8] This refers to both a physical death and a spiritual death. Scripture also tells us that "just as sin came into the world through one man, and death through sin, and so death spread to all men because all sinned."[9] This passage speaks of how all people physically die due to sin. But more significant than physical death is the consequence of spiritual death, which is being separated from God. The prophet Isaiah tells us that our "iniquities have made a separation between you and your God, and your sins have hidden His face from you so that He does not hear."[10] Since sin separates us from Him who gives and

---

[6] James 4:17.

[7] The topic of God's glory and our sin was largely explored in Chapter 2.

[8] Romans 6:23.

[9] Romans 5:12.

[10] Isaiah 59:2.

sustains our life, doesn't it make sense that physical death would follow? Thus, our physical death is a consequence of our spiritual death.

Nobody likes to hear that they are sinners, deserving of death and hell. Nevertheless, we are to proclaim God's truth, regardless of how uncomfortable it may be to share. If someone does not know they need to be saved, then they won't think they will need a savior. Sin is like a terminal illness and Jesus is the only cure, but a sick person who thinks that they are healthy will not take medicine to remedy the illness. It is only when someone comes to realize that they are a sinner in need of a savior that they will embrace Christ.

CHRIST: THE GOSPEL SOLUTION

It is only after we understand the bad news that we are able to appreciate and embrace the Good News, which is that Jesus came and died on our behalf. Scripture explains that:

> "You, who were dead in your trespasses and the uncircumcision of your flesh, God made alive together with Him, having forgiven us all our trespasses, by canceling the record of debt that stood against us with its legal demands. This he set aside, nailing it to the cross."[11]

While the punishment for rebellion against God is death, Jesus came from His heavenly throne to die the death that we deserved, to suffer the punishment that we incurred, and to give us a divine pardon for our treason. He did this on our behalf in order to redeem us from our captivity, to forgive us of our sin, and to restore our relationship with God. Jesus

---

[11] Colossians 2:13-14.

took our sins upon Himself while on the cross and in exchange He covered us with His righteousness. As Scripture states, "for our sake He made Him to be sin who knew no sin, so that in Him we might become the righteousness of God."[12] He took the penalty that we deserved to give us the eternal life that He earned.

We did not ask Him to do it, and in our sin, we rejected that it was even necessary. Read these passages of Scripture carefully:

> "While we were still weak, at the right time Christ died for the ungodly."[13]

> "God shows His love for us in that while we were still sinners, Christ died for us."[14]

> "For if while we were enemies we were reconciled to God by the death of His Son, much more, now that we are reconciled, shall we be saved by His life." [15]

Do you see God's love for us? While we were enemies of God, Jesus came to save us, by sacrificing His own life. Can you imagine dying to save the life of your enemy? Yet, while we were in open rebellion against the Lord of all Creation, Jesus died for us to save us from the just punishment that we deserved. He did this out of His great love for us. We did not deserve to be saved and we could not earn salvation since we are powerless to undo our sins. Yet, despite ourselves, God freely gives us salvation anyway, as Scripture explains, "for by grace you have been saved

---

[12] 2 Corinthians 5:21.
[13] Romans 5:6.
[14] Romans 5:8.
[15] Romans 5:10.

through faith. And this is not your own doing; it is the gift of God, not a result of works, so that no one may boast."[16]

The Good News of Christ gets better when we consider the resurrection. While Jesus died for our trespasses, He is not dead. On the third day, He rose from the grave and now sits at the right hand of God as the King of creation. In His resurrection, we can rest assured that Jesus is God in the flesh and His sacrificial atonement paid the debt of sin, freeing us from sin, and giving us eternal life.

RELATIONSHIP: THE PURSPOSE OF THE GOSPEL

The last element that we need to address when proclaiming the gospel is the purpose of the gospel. Why did Jesus forgive our sins? Why did He go through the torment of the cross? Yes, it was motivated out of love, but what did He achieve? What was the purpose?

Jesus tells us His purpose early in His ministry, stating that "God so loved the world, that He gave His only Son, that whoever believes in Him should not perish but have eternal life."[17] In His own words, Jesus came to save us from perishing in our sins and to give us eternal life. So the question is, what is eternal life? Is it simply to live forever? Is it to go to heaven?

Jesus answers this question at the end of His ministry, by stating, "this is eternal life, that they know you, the only true God, and Jesus Christ whom you have sent."[18] Jesus defines eternal life as knowing God. Again, it is not to know ABOUT God, nor is it to know OF God; rather, it is to KNOW God. Jesus is using relational language. Therefore, eternal life is about having a genuine relationship with God.

Since sin causes a separation between man and God, it should make sense that we have a restored relationship in the

---

[16] Ephesians 2:8-9.
[17] John 3:16.
[18] John 17:3.

atonement of Christ. Paul explains that "God has not destined us for wrath, but to obtain salvation through our Lord Jesus Christ, who died for us so that whether we are awake or asleep we might live with Him."[19] In this passage, Paul explains that Jesus died so that we would not suffer the due wrath of God. Jesus died so that we would live with Him. This is again relational language. The gospel is all about enjoying a restored relationship with God.

Eternal life is not about living forever. That is only a byproduct of having a relationship with God. We must be careful that we don't make the gospel about going to heaven, as if heaven is the focus. When we make heaven the focus of our message, we end up making an idol out of heaven. While it is true that Disciples of Christ will live forever and we will go to heaven (and later to the new heaven and new earth), these are only byproducts of having a restored relationship with God.

We do not want to make the opposite mistake either by making eternal life about escaping hell. While we want to be honest in sharing the horrors of hell, escaping hell should not be the focus of the gospel.

When we focus our message on living forever, or on the pleasures of heaven, or on the fear of hell, we are making the gospel centered on man rather than on God. Again, it is true that as Disciples of Christ we will live forever in new glorified bodies, it is true that we will enjoy life in the new heaven and new earth, and it is true that we will not suffer in hell; but these are all byproducts of the gospel, not the focus. The focus of the gospel should be centered on God's glory, on the work of Christ, and on the restored relationship that we now have due to the atonement of Christ on the cross.

This is an important element because it not only explains the purpose of the gospel (to bring us into relationship with God), but it also explains what our lives should look like now

---

[19] 1 Thessalonians 5:9-10.

131

that we have been adopted into God's family. When we realize that eternal life is about having a real relationship with God and that we have this restored relationship the moment that we have faith and trust in Christ, then we should realize that eternal life starts now. It is not some future event. As a Disciple of Christ, eternal life began the moment the Holy Spirit gave us new life. Thus, the gospel should impact how we live. In Christ, our sins have been washed away, and we are a new creation. Our lives should reflect our new life in Christ. Our relationship with Christ should drive our actions, thoughts, and motives.

PROCLAIM THE WHOLE GOSPEL

Simply put, when we share the gospel, we should declare that we are all sinners, separated from God, deserving of death, and doomed to suffer eternity in hell. Yet God loved us so much that He became a man to die on the cross, taking our sins upon Himself to satisfy the wrath of God. Jesus died on the cross to restore our relationship with God.

It is important that when we proclaim the gospel that we include all three points: Separation, Christ, and Relationship.

First, we begin by discussing the separation between God and man to set the stage for the Good News. This point establishes our condition without Christ and why we need a Savior. If we skip this point, then people will have a harder time understanding why they even need Jesus and will not understand the severity of sin nor the severity of God's justice.

We then transition to the cross. Christ crucified is the gospel, it is the main point. Christ is the heart and core of the gospel: Jesus dying on the cross for our sins is the gospel in the simplest form. If we skip this point, we skip the solution to our sin problem, not to mention we would be skipping the gospel itself. There is no gospel without Christ and Him crucified.

Concluding with the relational focus is the epilogue to the message. This final point addresses the purpose of the gospel and what life should look like as a Disciple of Christ. To skip this point will leave people thinking that all there is to be a Disciple of Christ is to believe in Jesus. While that is an essential element, it is only the beginning. People will not understand what life as a Disciple of Christ should look like if they do not understand that we now have a restored relationship with God through Christ. To ignore this element can hinder their spiritual growth as they will not seek to grow as an image bearer of Christ, nor will they grow in their relationship with Christ.

Even after providing these steps, some may still worry about exactly what to say when proclaiming the gospel. To those with this worry I encourage you to remember Jesus' words to His disciples as He prepared them to go throughout Judea to proclaim the kingdom of heaven. Jesus explained that His disciples would meet persecution and would be brought to the authorities. While that may be discouraging, Jesus encouraged His disciples by further explaining that, "when they deliver you over, do not be anxious how you are to speak or what you are to say, for what you are to say will be given to you in that hour. For it is not you who speak, but the Spirit of your Father speaking through you."[20] In these words, Jesus comforts us, stating the Holy Spirit, who is our Helper, will be with us and provide us with the very words that need to be said.

While we do not need to worry about what we will say and while it is true that the Holy Spirit will provide us the very words to express what God would have us express, this does not excuse us from the mandate to be prepared. While these two teachings may seem contradictory to each other, we can rest assured that God's word does not contradict

---

[20] Matthew 10:19-20; cross reference with Luke 12:11-12.

itself. Based on these two teachings, we can understand that we should be prepared, meaning that we should understand the essential elements of the gospel and be able to articulate it. At the same time, we should trust the Holy Spirit to provide the very words to articulate what needs to be said to any individual or group that we come across. We can be encouraged to know that we do not need to worry about exactly what we need to say. Therefore, I encourage you to use the three points of Separation, Christ, and Relationship as an outline to follow when proclaiming the gospel, while trusting the Holy Spirit to guide the conversation.

Chapter 13
Go For Christ: Bearer of Good News

EAGER TO GO

As ambassadors of Christ, we are bearers of the Good News. Sin is an illness that leads to death. The atoning sacrifice of Christ is the cure and, as Disciples of Christ, it is our responsibility and our privilege to share the Good News with others. We must remember that we too were once lost and doomed to eternal death; but God, full of mercy and grace, saved us.[1] Thus we should have compassion and love for those who do not know Christ and we should seek opportunities to proclaim the gospel. Furthermore, we should also remember that we did not come to know of God's grace on our own. There was likely someone in your life that God used to share the gospel with you. In hearing the Good News, God transformed our heart and adopted us into His family. As a member of God's family, as a citizen of the Holy Kingdom, and as an ambassador of Christ, we each now have the responsibility to share the Good News with others, just as someone once shared with us.

Once we have tasted the glory of God and experienced His goodness, we will desire to tell others of this wonderful news so that others may come to know Him and His glory. Think about what you do when you have good or exciting news. When we have good news or when something awesome happens to us, it is natural for people to want to tell

---

[1] Ephesians 2:1-5 states, "And you were dead in the trespasses and sins in which you once walked, following the course of this world, following the prince of the power of the air, and the spirit that is now at work in the sons of disobedience – among whom we all once lived in the passions of our flesh, carrying out the desires of the body and the mind, and were by nature children of wrath, like the rest of mankind. But God, being rich in mercy, because of the great love with which He loved us, even when we were dead in our trespasses, made us alive together with Christ – by grace you have been saved."

others about it. We love to talk about the things we love and there is no greater love than God's love for us.[2] When we experience His love and have truly tasted the salvation that we have in Christ, we will be compelled to tell others about God and His Good News.

Isaiah provides a great example for us when he was called to be a prophet of God. The prophet describes that he saw a vision of God sitting on a throne and angelic beings (called seraphim) were with God saying "Holy, holy, holy is the LORD of hosts; the whole earth is full of His glory!"[3] However, upon witnessing God's glory, Isaiah trembled, recognizing that he was not worthy to stand before God's perfect righteousness, calling out, "Woe is me! For I am lost; for I am a man of unclean lips, and I dwell in the midst of a people of unclean lips; for my eyes have seen the King, the LORD of hosts!"[4]

However, upon his acknowledgement of sin and repentant heart, God sent a seraph to purify Isaiah's unclean lips. He then explained to Isaiah that his guilt has been taken away and that his sins have been forgiven. After being forgiven, Isaiah heard God ask, "Whom shall I send, and who will go for us?" Then Isaiah answered, "Here I am! Send me."[5]

Notice that when Isaiah initially encountered the glory of God, he fell into fear and trembling, knowing that he was full of sin. However, God cleansed Isaiah of his sin. Then when God called for someone to go to the world on God's behalf, Isaiah was quick to volunteer. Having received salvation from God, Isaiah was eager to be God's messenger. Let us all follow Isaiah's example, let us all be just as eager to go out into the world to proclaim the gospel to the world.

---

[2] And there is no one that we should love more than God.

[3] Isaiah 6:3.

[4] Isaiah 6:5.

[5] Isaiah 6:8.

MESSENGERS, NOT SAVIORS

While I find great encouragement in Isaiah's call and eagerness to be sent on the behalf of God, there is more to Isaiah's story.[6] Once Isaiah responded to God's call, saying, "Here I am! Send me," God replied to Isaiah telling him:

> "Go, and say to this people: 'Keep on hearing, but do not understand; keep on seeing, but do not perceive. Make the heart of this people dull, and their ears heavy, and blind their eyes; lest they see with their eyes, and hear with their ears, and understand with their hearts, and turn and be healed.'"[7]

God's response to Isaiah's eagerness is not so encouraging, He told Isaiah that the people would reject the message. Isaiah would not have a thriving ministry; rather, his ministry would fall on deaf ears.

Isaiah then asked God, "How long, O Lord?"[8] Do you hear Isaiah's question? How long will the people reject the message? How long will my evangelical efforts be unsuccessful? How long must I preach to a people who will not respond? God answered Isaiah saying:

> "Until cities lie waste without inhabitant, and houses without people, and the land is a desolate waste, and the LORD removes

---

[6] When quoting Isaiah 6, most people tend to stop at verse 8 to encourage believers to also say, "Here I am! Send me." While this is encouraging, we should ensure that we read the rest of the chapter. God's response to Isaiah's eagerness and God's mission for Isaiah described in the rest of the chapter is important for us to understand.

[7] Isaiah 6:9-10.

[8] Isaiah 6:11.

people far away, and the forsaken places are many in the midst of the land."[9]

God's answer was just as discouraging. He told Isaiah that the people would reject the message for the entirety of Isaiah's time as a prophet. Yet, despite how discouraging God's responses may seem, Isaiah still went out and served as God's faithful prophet. What we learn from Isaiah's call and his ministry is that the measure of success is not in the numbers, it is not about how many respond positively to the message that we share. Rather, the measure of success is in our obedience to go where God has called us to go and say what God has called us to say, despite the hardship, obstacles, persecution, and lack of response.

As messengers of God, we are responsible for declaring God's truth and love to the world; we are not responsible with how people respond to the message. We are not called to save people. We do not have the ability to save others. We are not saviors. Jesus is the savior. Only God has the power to save. Our role is to point others to Him by proclaiming the gospel. A person's response to the message is between them and God. Sometimes people become discouraged in their evangelical efforts when they do not see a positive response. Some may think that they did something wrong or did not say the right thing or did not say it the right way. Do not take on that weight.

To help encourage you to not take this weight, I will remind you of two facts. First, as we share the Good News of Christ, we must remember that it is "by grace you have been saved through faith. And this is not your own doing; it is the gift of God, not a result of works, so that no one may

---

[9] Isaiah 6:11-12. God's answer to Isaiah is itself a prophecy that Israel (the northern kingdom) will be conquered by Assyria, which happens later in Isaiah's lifetime. God's answer could also refer to the fall of Judah (the southern kingdom), which happens about a hundred years after Isaiah's writings when Babylon conquered Judah.

boast."[10] Therefore, people are not saved by the works of man. We cannot work to earn someone else's salvation, not even when we might proclaim the gospel perfectly. Someone's conversion is not a burden we are called to bear.[11] We cannot change someone's heart; therefore, we are not responsible for how people respond to the gospel. We simply must faithfully proclaim the gospel.

Second, you don't know the seeds that you are planting. Even if a person reacts negatively or even repulsive to the gospel, that same person may come to faith later in life due to the seeds that God planted through you. You never know what seeds you are planting, and you may never know. It is about God's glory, not our own. We do not need credit, nor should we seek credit when someone embraces the gospel. The credit does not belong to us. We may have planted the seed, but it is God who causes the growth.[12]

Evangelism is simply declaring the Good News that Jesus came to die for our sins. Salvation is a work of God. Therefore, we cannot control who will respond positively to the gospel. Only God controls whether someone will embrace the gospel, as Jesus explained, "No one can come to me unless the Father who sent me draws him."[13]

We know that many people will reject the gospel. But why? Scripture tells us that "the word of the cross is folly to those who are perishing, but to us who are being saved it is the power of God."[14] Those who are perishing, those lost in their sin, think the gospel to be foolish and say that Disciples of Christ are fools for believing it. The gospel, the word of

---

[10] Ephesians 2:8-9.

[11] **Conversion:** "Our willing response to the gospel call, in which we sincerely repent of sins and place our trust in Christ for salvation" (Grudem, *Systematic Theology*, 861).

[12] 1 Corinthians 3:5-6 states, "What then is Apollos? What is Paul? Servants through whom you believed, as the Lord assigned to each. I planted, Apollos watered, but God gave the growth."

[13] John 6:44.

[14] 1 Corinthians 1:18.

the cross, will only make sense to those who are called to salvation, recognizing the power of God. Scripture goes on to say that "the natural person does not accept the things of the Spirit of God, for they are folly to him, and he is not able to understand them because they are spiritually discerned."[15] It is important to note that believing in the gospel is not something that we do by our own will. In our own will we all would reject the gospel as foolish. In our natural fallen state, we reject the teachings of the Holy Spirit as foolish nonsense. It is only by the power of the Holy Spirit that anyone can understand Scripture, it is only by the Spirit that anyone can understand the gospel, and it is only through the Spirit that anyone is able to respond positively to the Good News.

At this point, some might ask, "if I have no power to save someone, if it is all God, then why declare the gospel at all?" First, we are commanded by God to proclaim the gospel, thus we proclaim the gospel out of faithful obedience to our God.[16] Second, while it is God who changes hearts and causes people to receive the gospel, people still need to hear the gospel in order to respond to it. As Scripture states:

> "How then will they call on Him in whom they have not believed? And how are they to believe in Him of whom they have never heard? And how are they to hear without someone preaching? ... So faith comes from hearing, and hearing through the word of Christ."[17]

God has chosen to use His faithful followers to be the bearer of Good News. He then works in the hearts of people

---

[15] 1 Corinthians 2:14.
[16] Matthew 28:19-20, Mark 16:15, and Acts 1:8 are specifically about Jesus commanding His disciples to proclaim the gospel to the world.
[17] Romans 10:14, 17.

as the Good News is delivered. Our words do not have power in and of themselves, it is only when God empowers our words that they are able to transform rebellious hearts into God glorifying hearts. That being said, God uses His people to be His voice and share His words, which give life. This truth is demonstrated by the prophet Ezekiel when he was brought to a valley of dry bones. Bones have no life in them, yet God tells Ezekiel to speak to them. As impossible as that sounds, Ezekiel obeys and states the words provided by God:

> "O dry bones, hear the word of the LORD. Thus says the Lord GOD to these bones: Behold, I will cause breath to enter you, and you shall live. And I will lay sinews upon you, and will cause flesh to come upon you, and cover you with skin, and put breath in you, and you shall live, and shall know that I am the LORD."[18]

As Ezekiel spoke, the bones began to rattle and come together and then flesh began to cover the bones. After the bodies were formed, God provided Ezekiel more words to give the bodies life. Ezekiel records the results of obeying God's commands, stating, "So I prophesied as He commanded me, and the breath came into them, and they lived and stood on their feet, an exceedingly great army."[19]

God's vision to Ezekiel provides a great illustration of evangelism. We are called to speak to those still dead in their trespasses. Yet, it is only by the power and work of God that our words give life. God's words have power. It is by God's words that we were created. It is by God's words that we were recreated. This is why Paul can proclaim, "I am not ashamed of the gospel, for it is the power of God for

---

[18] Ezekiel 37:4-6.
[19] Ezekiel 37:10.

salvation to everyone who believes."[20] As we proclaim the gospel, we must trust in God's power to do the work, as God reveals to Isaiah, "so shall my word be that goes out from my mouth; it shall not return to me empty, but it shall accomplish that which I purpose, and shall succeed in the thing for which I sent it."[21]

Since the power is in God and in His word, we should trust in God's word and not in our own abilities of speech craft. We should follow Paul's example, who explains that when he came to Corinth, he came "to preach the gospel, and not with words of eloquent wisdom, lest the cross of Christ be emptied of its power."[22] He goes on to explain to the church stating:

> "And I, when I came to you, brothers, did not come proclaiming to you the testimony of God with lofty speech or wisdom. For I decided to know nothing among you except Jesus Christ and Him crucified. And I was with you in weakness and in fear and much trembling, and my speech and my message were not in plausible words of wisdom, but in demonstration of the Spirit and of power, so that your faith might not rest in the wisdom of men but in the power of God."[23]

Paul was a highly educated man, yet he did not attempt to use his worldly wisdom to persuade and manipulate people into believing. He simply taught others about "Christ and Him crucified." We should not try to convince people with fancy speech or charismatic tactics, instead we should trust God to speak for Himself through Scripture and prayer.

---

[20] Romans 1:16.
[21] Isaiah 55:11.
[22] 1 Corinthians 1:17.
[23] 1 Corinthians 2:1-5.

Chapter 14
Go For Christ: The Fear to Go

THE FEAR OF THE WHOLE TRUTH

We should not try to sugar coat God's truth. Jesus did not shy away from the hard teachings. In fact, we frequently see Jesus give some of His hardest teachings when particularly large crowds were following Him. The Gospel of Luke provides an example:

> "Now great crowds accompanied [Jesus] and He turned and said to them, 'If anyone comes to me and does not hate his father and mother and wife and children and brothers and sisters, yes, even his own life, he cannot be my disciple. Whoever does not bear his own cross and come after me cannot be my disciple. For which of you, desiring to build a tower, does not first sit down and count the cost, whether he has enough to complete it?"[1]

Did you read what Jesus said? He told the crowds that if they did not hate their parents, spouse, kids, siblings, and themselves, then they could not be His disciples. Can you imagine hearing that preached at an evangelistic event? Words like that do not "win souls."

When I first encountered this passage, I remember thinking to myself, "Jesus, what are you saying?" This is a hard teaching to digest and understand. Jesus' point was that God had to be first. Disciples of Christ must value Jesus over their own families. Speaking hard truths was what Jesus spoke about when large groups of people were following Him.

---

[1] Luke 14:25-28.

He goes on to say that to be a Disciple of Christ means bearing a cross. Many reading this book may think of the cross as a symbol of God's love for us (and it is). However, to those in Jesus' day, crucifixion was very real and those who heard Jesus' words would have thought of the cross as only an instrument of a torturous death. Telling potential disciples to "bear his own cross" would have been absurd and repulsive to hear. Those who heard Jesus' words would have understood that Jesus was telling them that they would have to put themselves to death. Again, this is a hard teaching that is difficult to understand.

To be a Disciple of Christ means to put to death our sinful desires, put to death our selfishness, and to put to death our old selves. Paul explains when we become a Disciple of Christ, our "old self was crucified with Him in order that the body of sin might be brought to nothing, so that we would no longer be enslaved to sin."[2] Paul is teaching the church that our old self, that is our sinful nature, was crucified with Christ. Therefore, in some sense each Disciple of Christ has taken the cross. In fact, Paul echoes this teaching in his letter to the Galatians stating that, "those who belong to Christ Jesus have crucified the flesh with its passions and desires."[3] To take up our cross daily, is to give up our old way of living, to live as a new creation in Christ, and to put to death our old self, which is the self that has already been crucified with Christ.

When Jesus told people "whoever does not bear his own cross and come after me cannot be my disciple," He wanted them to know that there would be sacrifice, suffering, and that you were either all in or not in at all. He was not interested in convincing them to follow Him, He wasn't willing to bend the truth, soften the truth, or state half-truths. He is only interested in speaking the truth. Jesus didn't just say what would be nice to hear. Jesus told people to count

---

[2] Romans 6:6.
[3] Galatians 5:24.

the cost, He wanted people to know up front what it meant to be a Disciple of Christ.

While most people liked the miracles that Jesus did, many did not like His teachings. When Jesus spoke boldly to the large crowds, many began to turn away. One example of this took place when Jesus fed over five thousand people with only five loaves of bread and two fish. Not only did Jesus feed everyone with so little, but there was plenty of leftovers after everyone was full. The people were miraculously well fed. At this point, thousands of people were following Jesus. This should not be surprising. He was healing them, casting out demons, turning water into high quality wine, and now providing free meals.

Then the next day, the people came to Jesus, but this time Jesus was not performing miracles, instead He turned to the crowd and taught them that He was the Bread of Life, which would certainly be a strange teaching to His hearers. Many in the group begin to think differently about Jesus and rejected this teaching. Nonetheless, they stayed to hear Him out. But Jesus' teachings become even more appalling. He went on to say, "I am the living bread that came down from heaven. If anyone eats of this bread, he will live forever. And the bread that I will give for the life of the world is my flesh."[4]

Did you read what Jesus just said? He again affirmed that He was the bread of life, but then goes on to say that they had to eat His flesh to have eternal life. While Jesus was speaking metaphorically, the people at the time did not understand what Jesus was talking about and were really only interested in His miracles.[5] But the crowds begin to dwindle when they realize that Jesus was not offering a free meal, He was only offering Himself. Scripture states that,

---

[4] John 6:51.
[5] Jesus was referring to how He was going to give His life and blood for the salvation of those who believe.

"after this many of His disciples turned back and no longer walked with Him."[6]

How does Jesus respond? Reflecting on this passage, Pastor Kyle Idleman wrote:

> "I was struck by the fact that Jesus doesn't chase after them. He doesn't soften his message to make it more appealing. He doesn't send the disciples chasing after them with a creative handout inviting them to come back for a 'build your own sundae' ice cream social. He seems okay with the fact that his popularity has plummeted."[7]

Jesus doesn't try to convince the crowd to stay. Instead, He turns to those who remained and asked, "Do you want to go away as well?"[8] For Jesus, it wasn't about the number of followers, it was about genuine followers.

Many of us want to be people pleasers, fearing that our crowds would leave if we taught the full truth; but we need to remember that it is not about us. We are not the object of worship. We should not be calling people to us. Rather, we should be pointing people to Him who created us, saved us, and worthy of all glory.

During His earthly ministry, Jesus was not interested in pleasing people, He was only interested in glorifying God with true disciples. He did all things for the glory of the Father, including dying on the cross on our behalf. Paul expressed similar sentiments when he wrote to the Galatians, "am I now seeking the approval of man, or of God? Or am I trying to please man? If I were still trying to please man, I would not be a servant of Christ."[9] We must have the same

---

[6] John 6:66.

[7] Idleman, *Not a Fan*, 13.

[8] John 6:67.

[9] Galatians 1:10.

mindset when we proclaim the gospel. While the gospel is indeed Good News… it is also offensive, and some will object to you sharing it. Yet, we share it, not to bring ourselves glory, nor to please people, but to bring glory to God.

THE FEAR OF MAN

During Jesus' earthly ministry, He sent out His disciples to proclaim to Israel that the Kingdom of God is at hand. He provided instructions on what they should do and how they should do it. He then warned them about being persecuted and encouraged them to not be afraid, stating to "not fear those who kill the body but cannot kill the soul. Rather fear Him who can destroy both soul and body in hell."[10] When talking about evangelism it is fitting to address the fear of man as it is usually the main cause that prevents us from declaring the gospel.

Admittedly, the fear of what man thinks of me is something that I struggled with greatly when I first became a Disciple of Christ (and still struggle with). I was uncomfortable talking about my faith to others due to the fear of what people would say or think. But early in my Christian life, a mentor of mine once said, "every time you meet with your non-Christian co-workers, friends, and family and you don't share the gospel you are basically telling them to have fun in hell."[11] I know that this statement can seem harsh, off-putting, and perhaps even offensive. To clarify, this hyperbole is not stating that we have the power to save others from hell; rather, it is meant to address the fear that we have in proclaiming the gospel to others.

Imagine having a friend who is sick with a terminal illness and imagine that you know the cure but refuse to share it with him. To do this is basically telling them to have

---

[10] Matthew 10:28.
[11] This is a paraphrase of my mentor Chaplain Jared Vineyard.

fun with their illness and letting them die. As Disciples of Christ, we are stewards of the very thing that can save others. Why do we refuse to share it? Why not offer them the very thing that can save them?

To be clear, we are not responsible for other people's salvation. It is not up to us how others will respond to the gospel. A person can only receive salvation through faith in Christ. We cannot force others to have faith. But we are God's instruments to teach His truth and are called to spread the word of salvation.

I have noticed an alarming growth of apathy and indifference among Christians toward non-Christians. We excuse this apathy by claiming that we don't want to hurt the relationships that we have with our non-Christian friends, or we fear what consequences may come from proclaiming Christ crucified. If this is a relationship that we genuinely care about, then that is all the more reason to have courage to declare God's truth. The most loving thing we can do is proclaim the gospel, for the gospel is the great testimony of God's love for us: God became flesh to die for our sins so that we can have an eternal relationship with Him.

Receiving the atonement of Christ is the only thing that can save us from the sickness of sin. We should not only be willing to share the cure, but we should have such a passion that we share the cure at every opportunity. Of course, we cannot make people take the medicine (for the medicine can only be received by faith), whether they accept it or not is between them and God. But we, as Disciples of Christ, need to repent of our apathy, indifference, and the fear of man. This repentance should lead us to deeply care about the salvation of others to the extent that we do something about it regardless of what others will think of us or do against us.

We should not let the fear of man triumph over the fear of God. For God is a God of justice, and the just punishment for sin is eternal damnation. The fear that our loved ones might suffer this punishment should outweigh our fear of their response to the gospel.

Fortunately, our God is also a God of love, and has provided a way for us to receive His righteousness, namely through faith in Jesus. As Disciples of Christ, we are servants of Christ the Lord; let us be faithful servants by proclaiming His truth.

Chapter 15
Go For Christ: Commissioned to Make Disciples

BREAKING DOWN THE GREAT COMMISSION

After Jesus' death and resurrection, He remained on earth for another forty days. During this time, He prepared His disciples to take the reins as He would soon ascend back to His throne. On the first day of His resurrection, Jesus revealed Himself to His disciples proving beyond a doubt that He was who He claimed to be (God) and that He accomplished His divine mission (redemption). Near the end of this time, Jesus gave His disciples one last command, stating:

> "All authority in heaven and on earth has been given to me. Go therefore and make disciples of all nations, baptizing them in the name of the Father and of the Son and of the Holy Spirit, teaching them to observe all that I have commanded you. And behold, I am with you always, to the end of the age."[1]

This passage is often referred to as the Great Commission because in this passage Jesus is commanding us to continue the mission. He wants us to spread the word of the gospel so that others may also come to know Him. Jesus expects His disciples to make disciples.

As we examine the Great Commission, we will notice that there are four interconnected directives. We can identify these directives when we examine the verbs within this commission: go, make, baptize, and teach. While many tend

---

[1] Matthew 28:18-20.

to focus on the word "go," the key command in this passage is actually, "make disciples." Notice that all the other commands are connected to the command "make disciples."[2] The purpose of our "going" is to make disciples, we are to baptize and teach the disciples that we made. Go, baptize, and teach all serve the command to "make disciples."

The command to make disciples has two inherent phases: evangelism and discipleship.

In the evangelism phase, Disciples of Christ focus their attention on those who do not yet know Christ by proclaiming the gospel. By sharing the gospel, the Holy Spirit will move some people to accept the call to Christ and thus some will become disciples. The evangelism phase fulfills the "go" and "make" commands of the Great Commission.

After the evangelism phase, we transition into the discipleship phase. In the discipleship phase, Disciples of Christ focus on those who are Disciples of Christ (to include the new convert). During this phase we are called to train, encourage, mentor, and help Disciples of Christ grow in their relationship with Christ and in their spiritual maturity. The discipleship phase fulfills the "baptize" and the "teach" command of the Great Commission.

The Great Commission is not only a call to evangelize; if we stop there then we are stopping short of our commission. Disciples of Christ can only be obedient to the Great Commission when we obey both phases. In both phases we are making disciples. In the evangelism phase we make disciples in the macro sense by calling people to become Disciples of Christ; whereas, in the discipleship phase we make disciples in the micro sense by taking on a

---

[2] While identifying the key verb as "make" may seem implicit in our English translations, it is clearly explicit in the Greek. In the original Greek, only the verb "make" is written in an imperative form, which means that it is the key command in this passage. The verbs go, baptize, and teach are supportive verbs, which serve to enhance our understanding of the key command. Thus, the command is to make disciples. Go, baptize, and teach is how we make disciples.

mentoring role in someone's life by walking alongside them to help them grow in Christ.

EVANGELISM PHASE

Generally, when we hear the command "Go," the question that we would likely ask is, "where are we going?" But Jesus doesn't have a specific location in mind when He gives His disciples this command. Instead of asking "where are we going," it would be more appropriate to ask "why are we going?" The key to the Great Commission is not so much about the destination, but the purpose. We are to go and make disciples.

A better translation of the Greek verb used in this passage is, "as you go." As Disciples of Christ, we are called to proclaim the gospel with the people we encounter *as we go* through life. Declaring the gospel to others is how we make disciples. We do not need to go to a different country or some far away land to obey the Great Commission. We can obey this command by simply proclaiming the gospel to people we encounter in our daily lives: our family, friends, coworkers, or people we happen to come across throughout our day.

We see a great example of this "as you go" approach to evangelism when Jesus traveled to Galilee by going through Samaria. While in Samaria, Jesus decided to take a pit stop at a nearby well and asked a woman for some water. Jesus was breaking traditions and cultural norms by making this request. At this time in history, Jews did not speak to Samaritans since they considered Samaritans as a second-class people. The woman replied to Jesus, "How is it that you, a Jew, ask for a drink from me, a woman of Samaria?"[3] Jesus takes this opportunity to transition the conversation to matters of deeper meaning. Suddenly, Jesus is talking to the

---

[3] John 4:9.

woman about "living water" and "eternal life." The conversation ends with the woman embracing Jesus as the promised Messiah. Jesus just came for some water and instead made a disciple. How did He do this?

First, Jesus always has His mission in mind. Regardless of what He is doing at the time, who He is talking to, or how tired He may be, He is always mindful of opportunities to share the gospel.

Second, He initiated the conversation. For many people, initiating the conversation is the hardest part. To talk to a Samaritan woman would have been awkward and counter cultural; but Jesus was not interested in what people thought, rather He was interested in people's eternal state. It can be awkward and even a bit scary to start the conversation; yet, once the conversation begins, it can grow into something meaningful.

Third, Jesus did not stay at the surface level. He intentionally transitioned the conversation to matters of eternal importance. We can't be afraid of going to the deep and meaningful.

Lastly, Jesus showed that He had specific knowledge about the woman by pointing out that the woman had previously had five husbands and the man she was currently with was not her husband. This example shows that we need to take time to know our audience. Though Jesus likely knew what He knew due to His divine nature, we have the Holy Spirit (who is equally divine) living in us. We must trust in the Holy Spirit to guide us. Trust that He will give us insight, discernment, and the words to say. Trust in the mission that God has given us. Always ready for the mission, even when all we are trying to do is get a cup of water.

While we do not need to travel to distant lands to obey the Great Commission, going on a mission trip to proclaim the gospel to other nations is certainly within the scope of the Great Commission. When stating the Great Commission,

Jesus commanded His disciples to "make disciples of all nations." All people from all places need to hear the gospel. In His final words to His disciples, Jesus stated, "You will receive power when the Holy Spirit has come upon you, and you will be my witnesses in Jerusalem and in all Judea and Samaria, and to the end of the earth."[4] Jesus has a global mission in mind in stating this command.

We see a great example of mission trips in the life of Paul. Scripture records that he went on three different journeys to proclaim the gospel beyond the Israel boarders. Yet the same principles that we see with Jesus at the well applies during these trips as well.

As Paul traveled, He went from country to country, preaching the gospel to anyone who would listen. While doing so, Paul took the time to learn about His audience. A great example of this was when He traveled to Athens. While he was in the Greek city, Paul took the time to understand the culture and noticed that they had shrines for many different God's to include an unknown God. Eventually, Paul was invited to speak to a large audience of well-respected men of the city. Paul used his knowledge about these people as a base to build his case for the gospel stating:

> "Men of Athens, I perceive that in every way you are very religious. For as I passed along and observed the objects of your worship, I found also an altar with this inscription: 'To the unknown god.' What therefore you worship as unknown, this I proclaim to you. The God who made the world and everything in it, being Lord of heaven and earth, does not live in temples made by man, nor is He served by human hands, as though He needed

---

[4] Acts 1:8.

anything, since He Himself gives to all mankind life and breath and everything."[5]

He then goes on to say:

"Being then God's offspring, we ought not to think that the divine being is like gold or silver or stone, an image formed by the art and imagination of man. The times of ignorance God overlooked, but now He commands all people everywhere to repent, because He has fixed a day on which He will judge the world in righteousness by a man whom He has appointed; and of this He has given assurance to all by raising Him from the dead."[6]

Paul used what he knew about the Greeks to begin his teachings, which helped establish Paul as credible and provided his audience a basis to follow along his teachings. He then explained that the God he was proclaiming was a God they were unknowingly already worshipping. Paul then began to teach the truth of God, by explaining that God was the creator of all things and even addressed how creating idols did not make sense, since God is the creator.

He then concluded by calling the audience to repent and to believe in the one whom God had appointed and resurrected. In response, some who listened to Paul mocked him, while others said that they wanted Paul to come back and share more about this God. Some even believed Paul and joined him.

Paul took the time to understand his audience, remained respectful to his audience, yet still boldly proclaimed the gospel. He shared the truth with love.

---

[5] Acts 17:22-25.
[6] Acts 17:29-31.

There are some noticeable differences in Jesus' approach in Samaria and Paul's approach in Athens. Jesus was just passing through Samaria and found Himself in a conversation with a woman at a well, whereas Paul deliberately traveled to other nations to preach the gospel. While Jesus relied on divine knowledge to approach the woman about her sin, Paul took time to understand the culture of his audience. Yet, while we see a contrast in the specific methods that Jesus and Paul used, we must not think one method is right and the other wrong. This teaches us that we are called to preach the gospel to anyone we happen to meet.

There may be times that we are called to go out to other nations. At other times we may be called to stay in the local area and preach to our neighbors. There may be times that we should take time to understand our audience before we evangelize. At other times we may be compelled by the Spirit to jump right in without knowing anything about the person, trusting in the Spirit for wisdom and insight. Either way, we know that the Spirit is at work, guiding our words. While we may see a difference in how Jesus and Paul evangelized, the primary thing that Jesus and Paul had in common was that they had the mission on the forefront of their mind ready to go as they went out.

DISCIPLESHIP PHASE

Proclaiming the gospel is only the first half of the Great Commission. Once someone responds positively to the gospel, it is important to follow through with discipleship. Jesus describes the conversion experience as being born again.[7] New Disciples of Christ begin their walk as infants in the faith. Just as we would not leave a newborn infant to

---

[7] John 3:3 states, "Jesus answered him, 'Truly, truly, I say to you, unless one is born again he cannot see the kingdom of God.'"

fend for themselves, it would be just as irresponsible for the church to not care for a new disciple.

It is imperative that we help guide the new convert in their journey as a Disciple of Christ. While discipleship is important for all Disciples of Christ, it is particularly important for a new believer, as they are newborn infants in the faith. Therefore, they need a little more deliberate discipleship to help them understand their new identity in Christ, to help them grow in their relationship with God, and to help solidify the foundational truths on which they are learning to stand.

Notice that immediately after Jesus commands His disciples to make disciples, He commands them to ensure that new disciples are baptized. This illustrates that baptism is important and should be one of the first commands that new disciples obey.

As mentioned earlier in this book, baptism is a ceremony where a person declares their new identity in Christ to the world. It is a declaration that they have been born again into a new life. Scripture states:

> "Do you not know that all of us who have been baptized into Christ Jesus were baptized into His death? We were buried therefore with Him by baptism into death, in order that, just as Christ was raised from the dead by the glory of the Father, we too might walk in newness of life."[8]

In baptism we are submerged under water, representing how our sinful self has been put to death and buried with Christ. Just as Christ rose from the grave in His resurrection, we come back up from the water to represent our new life in

---

[8] Romans 6:3-4.

Christ. Baptism is a visual and ceremonial representation of being born again.

How does a Disciple of Christ help nurture a new disciple's growth? Peter addresses this question by stating, "like newborn infants, long for the pure spiritual milk, that by it you may grow up into salvation – if indeed you have tasted that the Lord is good."[9] Peter echoes the "newborn" analogy to describe new Christians. He then goes on to say that just as newborns need milk (as opposed to solid food), new disciples need spiritual milk to grow.

What is this spiritual milk? Scripture explains that spiritual milk is "the basic principles of the oracles of God."[10] Therefore we can provide spiritual milk when we teach others about the truth and love of God. This brings us to the final command within the Great Commission. After telling us to go, make, and baptize disciples, Jesus commands us to "teach them to observe all that I have commanded you."[11]

Discipleship is about teaching, training, helping, and mentoring other people to grow in Christ, where we come along side someone on their journey and invest in their relationship with God. The hope is that those who we disciple will grow beyond milk that they may be able to eat solid food. That they may grow in Christ and in maturity in their faith.

There is nothing wrong with spiritual milk as a new Disciple of Christ. It is part of the process of growing in Christ. Eventually the new disciple should be able to eat solid food. However, the danger is when Disciples of Christ do not spiritually grow beyond drinking milk and become stagnant in their faith.

Consider these warnings from Scripture:

---

[9] 1 Peter 2:2-3.
[10] Hebrews 5:12.
[11] Matthew 28:20.

"But I, brothers, could not address you as spiritual people, but as people of the flesh, as infants in Christ. I fed you with milk, not solid food, for you were not ready for it."[12]

"For though by this time you ought to be teachers, you need someone to teach you again the basic principles of the oracles of God. You need milk, not solid food, for everyone who lives on milk is unskilled in the word of righteousness, since he is a child. But solid food is for the mature, for those who have their powers of discernment trained by constant practice to distinguish good from evil."[13]

To clarify, discipleship is not only for new believers. In fact, just as all Disciples of Christ are called to make disciples, each Disciple of Christ should also seek mentorship from another Disciple of Christ. Each of us, regardless of how spiritually mature we may be, should look for mentors to disciple us as we disciple others. In this life we will never stop growing in Christ, and thus we can always learn from someone.

Furthermore, while it may seem natural and ideal that you would disciple the person that came to Christ through you, this is not always the case. God may use you to proclaim the gospel, then God may use someone else to disciple and nurture the new convert. Likewise, you may be called to disciple a new Disciple of Christ, even though you were not the one God used in their conversion.

Consider Paul's words to the Corinthians when he stated, "I planted, Apollos watered, but God gave the growth."[14]

---

[12] 1 Corinthians 3:1-2.
[13] Hebrews 5:12-14.
[14] 1 Corinthians 3:6.

Paul was the one that came to Corinth and shared the gospel, which planted the seeds of faith by which people came to believe in Christ. Sometime later, Apollos came to Corinth and taught the Corinthian believers, continuing the work that Paul started. Yet, Paul did not feel as though he was in competition with Apollos, rather he recognized that their work complemented each other and that they were on the same team, being used by God to accomplish the same goal. The human work of evangelism and discipleship is in reality God's work and it is God who ultimately causes the growth. We must always remember God uses His people to help others grow, yet only the power of God can cause growth.

So, how do we help others grow? What should we be teaching them? Consider the things that helped you grow and the things that are currently helping you grow. Those same things will likely help others grow as well. Jesus tells us to teach them to observe all that He has commanded; therefore, we should teach them the commands of Jesus.

Teach them that we were created to give **glory** to God and that we were saved into a relationship with God to fulfill this purpose. Help them understand their identity in Christ, the relationship they have with God, reminding them about the gospel, and encouraging them to consider how their life should reflect this new life that we have in Christ. Encourage them to be honest about their temptations and struggle with sin. Remind them that Christ has called them out of their sin, freeing them from their sin, and has "cleansed us from all unrighteousness."[15] Remind them that God has created us for His glory and encourage them to do all things for the glory of God.

Teach others to **grow** in their relationship and identity in Christ. As discussed earlier in this book, Scripture reading, prayer, and fellowship are the three pillars of growth.

---

[15] 1 John 1:9 states, "If we confess our sins, He is faithful and just to forgive us our sins and to cleanse us from all unrighteousness."

Therefore, we help others grow by encouraging them to read Scripture, engaging them in discussion about what they read, asking them to explain what they read, and encouraging them to memorize Scripture. We help others grow by teaching others to pray, encouraging them to pray every day in personal quiet time and praying together out loud. We help others through our relationship and fellowship by:

- Spending one on one time with those whom we disciple.
- Sharing our personal life with them.
- Inviting them to share their personal life with you.
- Sharing your testimony about your conversion and current walk with Christ.
- Inviting them to share their testimony about their conversion and current walk with Christ.
- Sharing your struggles and temptations.
- Inviting them to share their struggles and temptations.
- Inviting them to a church body to worship, read Scripture, and pray in fellowship with other disciples.

Also, we help others grow by checking in with them to see how they are doing, by holding them accountable for their self-training, and by coming alongside them asking how can we help in their growth.

Teach them that they too are called to **go** and make disciples. Explain to them they are now no longer of the world and that they are a citizen of the Kingdom of God living in this world as an ambassador of Christ. Teach them how to articulate the gospel and encourage them to be faithful bearers of the Good News.

Consider Paul's words to Timothy, "what you have heard from me in the presence of many witnesses entrust to faithful men who will be able to teach others also."[16] Paul is instructing Timothy to teach others who will in turn teach others. Jesus wants us to make disciples who will make disciples.

In short, we are to teach fellow Disciples of Christ to give Glory to Christ, Grow in Christ, and Go for Christ.

G **O**	**"GO therefore and make disciples of all nations, baptizing them in the name of the Father and of the Son and of the Holy Spirit, teaching them to observe all that I have commanded you. And behold, I am with you always, to the end of the age."** **~Matthew 28:19-20** • What is the gospel? Why is it important to proclaim the gospel? • Are you living your life as an Ambassador of Christ? Are you declaring the gospel? • How do we make disciples? What is our role when someone professes Christ as their Lord and God?

*** PAUSE HERE TO PRAYFULLY REFLECT ON THE ABOVE PASSAGE & QUESTIONS***

---

[16] 2 Timothy 2:2.

Conclusion
Three Words, One Message

"I appeal to you therefore, brothers, by the mercies of God, to present your bodies as a living sacrifice, holy and acceptable to God, which is your spiritual worship. Do not be conformed to this world, but be transformed by the renewal of your mind, that by testing you may discern what is the will of God, what is good and acceptable and perfect."
~ Romans 12:1-2

THREE WORDS

I hope this book has helped you better understand what it means to be a Disciple of Christ and that you would apply this understanding into your daily life. While much was discussed in this book, it can all be summarized with three simple words: Glory, Grow, Go.

I encourage you to take a moment to reflect on how these three words relate to living life as a Disciple of Christ. As you reflect on these three words, consider the key Scripture passage associated with each word:

GLORY
"So, whether you eat or drink, or whatever you do, do all to the glory of God."
~ 1 Corinthians 10:31

GROW
"Rather, speaking the truth in love, we are to grow up in every way into Him who is the head, into Christ"
~Ephesians 4:15

GO

"Go therefore and make disciples of all nations, baptizing them in the name of the Father and of the Son and of the Holy Spirit, teaching them to observe all that I have commanded you. And behold, I am with you always, to the end of the age."
~ Matthew 28:19-20

*** PAUSE HERE TO PRAYFULLY REFLECT ON THE ABOVE PASSAGES ***

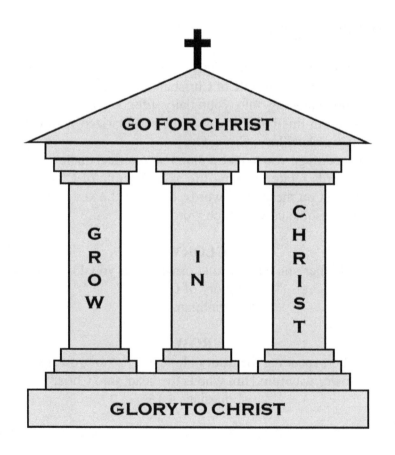

Throughout this book I have used a picture of a building to illustrate different aspects of the life of a Disciple of Christ. Previously, we have looked at each of these pieces individually, but now let us relook at each piece and consider how they fit together.

GLORY: Praising God, honoring God, and glorifying God is the foundation on which defines who we are as Disciples of Christ, everything else should be built on this foundation. Giving glory to God should govern all that we do, all that we say, all that we think, and all that we are. The foundational purpose for our creation is to glorify God. Yet, sin separated us from God, and destroyed this foundation. Christ then came and restored our relationship with God by dying on the cross. With our relationship restored, our foundation has been rebuilt. Therefore, in our salvation, glorifying God should define who we are as Disciples of Christ. Furthermore, our capacity to grow is dependent on the strength and solidity of this foundation. The stronger the foundation, the more that can be built on that foundation and the more that we are able to grow in Christ.

GROW: Built on the foundation are the three Pillars of Growth: Scripture, prayer, and fellowship. Each of these pillars are essential to the framework. If even one of these pillars is missing, the building will topple over and collapse. While the foundation may remain steady, we will not grow without the three pillars. Our time in Scripture, in prayer, and in fellowship directly impacts our growth. To be clear, it is God who causes the growth; yet God uses Scripture, prayer, and fellowship as the primary source of spiritual nutrients. They are the building blocks that God uses for our spiritual growth. Yet, since it is God who causes the growth, Scripture, prayer, and fellowship only work when they are built on the foundation of giving glory to God and enjoying our relationship with Him. The height of our metaphorical building is determined by the height of these three pillars; therefore, the more we receive nutrients from Scripture, prayer, and fellowship, the more these pillars will grow. When the pillars grow, then the building becomes taller, which resembles our spiritual growth.

GO: The top of the building is the roof. Placed on top of the roof is the cross of Christ serving as a beacon to call others to Him. The taller the building, the more it stands out above the buildings of the world, which will enable others to see the cross. From a distance, the first thing that people notice about a building is the top of the building; likewise, the first things people will notice about us is how we use our time, how we serve others, and our willingness to give to others. Yet, we must remember that our works should not be pointing to ourselves, it should be pointing to the cross. Therefore, we should use our works as opportunities to proclaim Christ and declare the gospel to others. Thus, our building illustration has the cross at the top of the building, the place of prominence, which should draw the attention and focus of others. Jesus tells His disciples that they "are the light of the world. A city set on a hill cannot be hidden. Nor do people light a lamp and put it under a basket, but on a stand, and it gives light to all in the house. In the same way, let your light shine before others, so that they may see your good works and give glory to your Father who is in heaven."[1] Jesus is explaining that the work of the disciple is to serve as a light, as a beacon, to call others to Him.

THE FLOW: Glory to Christ is the foundation on which we grow. The more we focus on the glory of God and live to bring Him glory, the more we will grow in our relationship with Him and grow in our identity in Christ. As we grow in Christ, we will be driven to tell others, thus we will go for

---

[1] Matthew 5:14-16.

Christ. Also, the more we grow in our identity in Christ, the more we are equipped to go and proclaim the gospel to others. Therefore, the more we bring glory to Christ, the more we grow in Christ. The more we grow in Christ, the more we are driven and enabled to go for Christ. Thus, we see a flow in which glory drives our growth, and our growth drives our motivation and ability to go.

INTERCONNECTED RELATIONSHIP

While the primary flow is Glory to Grow to Go, we also see an interconnected flow as well. Do not make the mistake in thinking that we should wait to focus on our spiritual growth until we sufficiently align our life to the glory of God, if this were the case then we would never focus on our growth. Likewise, it is not that we wait to go for God until we have reached a certain level of growth in Christ, if this were the case then we would never go.

GROW AND GO POINTS BACK TO GLORY: Glorifying God should transcend into all of who we are and all of what we do, thus our growing and going should be built on the foundation of giving glory to God. The more we grow in Christ, the more we will understand the depths of God's goodness and love, which will drive us to further glorify God. We glorify God as we go and proclaim God's glory to others. Yet, not only is declaring the gospel, God's truth, and God's love to others an act of glorifying God, but it will also drives us into adoration and bring the glory of God to the forefront of our mind. Furthermore, as we go and proclaim the gospel to others, we are calling others to know and glorify God, as Scripture states, "as grace extends to more and more people it may increase thanksgiving, to the glory of God".[2] We should grow in Christ and go for Christ in a way that brings glory to Christ. Therefore, growing in Christ and going for Christ are ways that we glorify Christ.

GO POINTS BACK TO GROW: Just as growing and going feed back into glory, going for Christ also feeds back into our growing. As we go and make disciples, we are often put in uncomfortable situations. For many, proclaiming the gospel itself is uncomfortable and could result in suffering consequences. Yet doing something outside our comfort zone is how we grow and is sign of growth. God uses suffering as a tool to help us grow. In fact Scripture tells us to "count it all joy, my brothers, when you meet trials of various kinds, for you know that the testing of your faith produces steadfastness. And let steadfastness have its full effect, that you may be perfect and complete, lacking in nothing."[3] Times of trial, hardship, suffering, or simply being uncomfortable are times that we depend all the more on God for guidance and direction to accomplish His will. As we learn to depend on God in all things, we grow in our relationship with Him. Therefore, whatever consequence we suffer in proclaiming the gospel will only serve to help us grow in Christ.

Furthermore, as we make disciples, we are teaching others about the truth and love of God. As we teach others, we are reminded of God's truth and love ourselves, and thus also impacts our growth. One of the best ways to learn is to teach, and as we learn more about God's love and truth, the more we grow to appreciate God's goodness and grow closer to Him.

---

[2] 2 Corinthians 4:15.
[3] James 1:2-4; cross reference with Romans 5:3-5.

While it is true that glory drives our growth, and that our growth drives our going, we must also understand that these three aspects are also interconnected and reinforce each other to some degree. Therefore, as Disciples of Christ, we are called to simultaneously give glory to God, grow in Christ, and go for Christ.

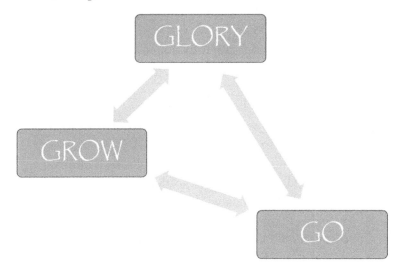

ONE MESSAGE

I hope understanding the Glory-Grow-Go concept provides clarity and serves as a helpful guide in your walk as a Disciple of Christ. While exploring each little nuance of being a Disciple of Christ can be helpful, it can also be overwhelming. Our minds can easily get stuck in the details and lose the bigger picture. To help prevent this from happening, we just need to remember one thing: embrace the relationship.

Being a Disciple of Christ is about enjoying a genuine relationship with God. Restoring our relationship with God is THE reason that Jesus died on the cross for our sins.

It is our relationship with God that drives the Glory-Grow-Go model. In fact, glorifying God, growing in Christ, and going for Christ are all products of our relationship with God. While I encourage you to be deliberate and mindful to glorify God, grow in Christ, and proclaim the gospel wherever you go; it is only when we embrace our relationship with God and our identity in Christ that we are able and willing to do so.

When we focus our attention on our relationship with God and our identity in Christ, then we will be driven to:

- Glorify God in all that we do
- Read His word
- Go to Him in prayer
- Fellowship with other disciples as a family
- Proclaim the gospel so that others may come to know Christ as well

The key to it all is to embrace your relationship with God in a way that gives Him glory.

"And this is eternal life, that they know you, the only true God, and Jesus Christ whom you have sent."
~ John 17:3

Appendix A
References & Recommended Reading

The below list of publications are books that I either quoted directly from or paraphrased. I recommend all Disciples of Christ to read these books as well.

Driscoll, Mark. *Who Do You Think You Are?: Finding Your True Identity in Christ*. Nashville, TN: Thomas Nelson, 2013.

Grudem, Wayne A. *Systematic Theology: an Introduction to Biblical Doctrine*. Second ed. Grand Rapids, MI: Zondervan Academic, 2020.

Idleman, Kyle. *Not a Fan. Becoming a Completely Committed Follower of Jesus*. Grand Rapids, MI: Zondervan, 2011.

Keller, Timothy, and Kathy Keller. *The New City Catechism: 52 Questions and Answers for Our Hearts and Minds*. Wheaton, Il: Crossway, 2017.

Neighbour, Ralph W., and Bill Latham. *Survival Kit: Five Keys to Effective Spiritual Growth*. Nashville, TN: LifeWay Press, 1996.

Sproul, R. C. "The Westminster Shorter Catechism." In *Truths We Confess: a Systematic Exposition of the Westminster Confession of Faith*. Orlando, Fl: Reformation Trust, 2019.

Vanderstelt, Jeff. *Gospel Fluency: Speaking the Truths of Jesus into the Everyday Stuff of Life*. Wheaton, Il: Crossway, 2017.

Appendix B
Helpful Resources

Throughout this book, I have provided what I hope to be helpful aids and resources. To make it a bit easier to review these learning aids, I have compiled them into this appendix so that they can be easily accessible in one location. My intention is that this appendix would be a helpful quick reference tool. Additionally, I have provided a selection of Bible reading plans.

1. PILLARS OF GROWTH

Scripture Reading: Reading our Bible is the primary way that God talks to us. Also, it is a great way to learn more about Him and get to know Him! Scripture is a crucial tool that God uses to cause spiritual growth. See chapter 7 for more information.

Prayer: I find it extremely comforting that we can talk to God anytime; in fact, He wants us to come to Him and tell Him about our day (both the good and the bad). I strongly encourage all Disciples of Christ to make prayer a daily part of their life. See chapter 8 for more information.

Fellowship: Being united with other Christians is especially important as we grow in our faith. We can encourage each other, help each other, teach each other, and worship God together. We need to remember that all Christians are together one family and God is our Father! See chapter 9 for more information.

2. HOW TO READ THE BIBLE: LISTEN, LEARN, LIVE

LISTEN
- KEY QUESTION: What does the passage say?
- Summarize or outline the passage.
- Note repeating words and repeating themes.

LEARN
- KEY QUESTION: What does the passage mean?
- What is the point of the text?
- Interview the text by asking the five W's: Who, What, When, Where, Why?
- Does this passage relate to other passages of the Bible?

LIVE
- KEY QUESTION: How can you apply the passage in your life?
- Is there a truth that should influence what you believe, how you feel, or how you behave?
  - o Is there a command to obey? Is there a promise to cling to? Is there an example to follow?
  - o Is there a sin to avoid?
- Conduct an alignment check on your heart:
  - o Do you embrace this truth in your mind, heart, and life?
  - o Are there areas in your life where you are not submitting to the truths revealed in the passage? If so, what is causing you to stumble (what idol are you clinging to)?
  - o How is God using this passage to transform you into His righteousness?
- Share: Who does God want you to share this with?

See chapter 7 (pages 77-78) for more information.

3. GUIDE TO DAILY SCRIPTURE READING

1) NECESSITY. Recognize that reading Scripture is a necessity for your spiritual growth, just as food is a necessity to your physical growth.

2) DEDICATE TIME. Designate a set time to spend one on one time with God in His Word and in prayer.

3) DAILY. Get into the word each day to spend time with God. Quality over quantity is the key during your daily time in the word.

4) GUARD YOUR HEART. Guard your heart from becoming legalistic in this discipline.

5) PRAY. Before you read, I encourage you to pray to God and ask the Holy Spirit to grant you focus, understanding, and to have your mind and heart transformed as you read.

6) VERSE BY VERSE. When you start a book of the Bible, start at chapter one and continue through each chapter until you finish the book.

7) FOR THE GLORY OF GOD. Read to glorify God and to grow in relationship with Him. Let this be the heart-motivation that drives you to the word of God.

See chapter 7 (pages 79-80) for more information.

4. A.C.T.S. MODEL OF PRAYER

ADORATION: Reflect on the character and attributes of God.

CONFESSION: Confess and repent of your sins.

THANKSGIVING: Reflect on the many blessings that God has given us.

SUPPLICATION: Let your requests be made known.

See chapter 8 (pages 83-88) for more information.

5. FOUR T'S OF GIVING

TIME: Volunteering time is one of our most valuable resources to give.

TALENT: Using our gifts, abilities, and skills to serve others.

TREASURE: Giving material objects to help others (money, food, resources, etc.).

TESTIMONY: Give your eyewitness account of God's glory and blessings. Be sure to proclaim the Gospel.

See chapter 11 for more information.

6. HOW TO DECLARE THE GOSPEL

SEPARATION: THE NEED FOR THE GOSPEL
- Define sin.
- Explain that all are sinners.
- Explain that due to sin we are separated from God.

CHRIST: THE GOSPEL SOLUTION
- God became man, Jesus.
- Jesus died on the cross to take the punishment of our sins and to cover us with His righteousness.
- Jesus was resurrected.

RELATIONSHIP: THE PURPOSE OF THE GOSPEL
- Through Christ, our relationship with God has been reconciled.
- Eternal life is about enjoying a real relationship with God.
- This restored relationship occurs the moment we have faith in Christ and should impact how we live the rest of our lives.

See chapter 12 for more information.

7. BIBLE READING PLANS

In this section I have provided three different reading plans. You can start with any of these or find one online. There are multiple free resources for those who want to dig into God's word.
- New Testament Reading Plan
- Cover to Cover Reading Plan
- Chronological Reading Plan

NEW TESTAMENT READING PLAN

This is a simple reading plan to read through the New Testament. In this plan you will read the New Testament in 105 days, reading about two to three chapters a day.

Day	Book	Chapters	Day	Book	Chapters	Day	Book	Chapters
1	Luke	1-2	36	Colossians	1-2	71	Hebrews	4-5
2	Luke	3-4	37	Colossians	3-4	72	Hebrews	6-7
3	Luke	5-6	38	Ephesians	1-3	73	Hebrews	8-9
4	Luke	7-8	39	Ephesians	4-6	74	Hebrews	10-11
5	Luke	9-10	40	Philippians	1-2	75	Hebrews	12-13
6	Luke	11-12	41	Philippians	3-4	76	James	1-2
7	Luke	13-14	42	1 Corinthians	1-3	77	James	3-5
8	Luke	15-16	43	1 Corinthians	4-6	78	Jude	1
9	Luke	17-18	44	1 Corinthians	7-9	79	Mark	1-2
10	Luke	19-20	45	1 Corinthians	10-11	80	Mark	3-4
11	Luke	21-22	46	1 Corinthians	12-14	81	Mark	5-7
12	Luke	23-24	47	1 Corinthians	15-16	82	Mark	8-10
13	Acts	1-2	48	2 Corinthians	1-4	83	Mark	11-13
14	Acts	3-4	49	2 Corinthians	5-7	84	Mark	14-16
15	Acts	5-6	50	2 Corinthians	8-10	85	1 Peter	1-2
16	Acts	7-8	51	2 Corinthians	11-13	86	1 Peter	3-5
17	Acts	9-10	52	1 Thessalonians	1-2	87	2 Peter	1-3
18	Acts	11-12	53	1 Thessalonians	3-5	88	John	1-3
19	Acts	13-14	54	2 Thessalonians	1-3	89	John	4-6
20	Acts	15-16	55	Titus	1-3	90	John	7-9
21	Acts	17-18	56	1 Timothy	1-3	91	John	10-12
22	Acts	19-20	57	1 Timothy	4-6	92	John	13-15
23	Acts	21-22	58	2 Timothy	1-2	93	John	16-18
24	Acts	23-24	59	2 Timothy	3-4	94	John	19-21
25	Acts	25-26	60	Matthew	1-2	95	1 John	1-3
26	Acts	27-28	61	Matthew	3-4	96	1 John	4-5
27	Galatians	1-3	62	Matthew	5-7	97	2 & 3 John	1&1
28	Galatians	4-6	63	Matthew	8-10	98	Revelation	1-3
29	Romans	1-3	64	Matthew	11-13	99	Revelation	4-6
30	Romans	4-6	65	Matthew	14-16	100	Revelation	7-9
31	Romans	7-9	66	Matthew	17-19	101	Revelation	10-12
32	Romans	10-12	67	Matthew	20-22	102	Revelation	13-15
33	Romans	13-14	68	Matthew	23-25	103	Revelation	16-18
34	Romans	15-16	69	Matthew	26-28	104	Revelation	19-20
35	Philemon	1	70	Hebrews	1-3	105	Revelation	21-22

COVER TO COVER READING PLAN

Read the whole Bible in a year from cover to cover. This reading plan starts at the beginning with the first book of the Bible, Genesis. Then continues book by book all the way to the last book of the Bible, Revelation.

Day	Reading	Day	Reading	Day	Reading
1	Gen 1-3	41	Lev 21-23	81	Jdg 1-3
2	Gen 4-7	42	Lev 24-25	82	Jdg 4-5
3	Gen 8-11	43	Lev 26-27	83	Jdg 6-7
4	Gen 12-15	44	Num 1-2	84	Jdg 8-9
5	Gen 16-18	45	Num 3	85	Jdg 10-12
6	Gen 19-21	46	Num 4-6	86	Jdg 13-15
7	Gen 22-24	47	Num 7	87	Jdg 16-18
8	Gen 25-26	48	Num 8-10	88	Jdg 19
9	Gen 27-29	49	Num 11-13	89	Jdg 20-21; Rut 1
10	Gen 30-31	50	Num 14-15	90	Rut 2-4
11	Gen 32-33	51	Num 16-17	91	1 Sa 1-3
12	Gen 34-36	52	Num 18-20	92	1 Sa 4-7
13	Gen 37-39	53	Num 21-22	93	1 Sa 8-9
14	Gen 40-41	54	Num 23-25	94	1 Sa 10-13
15	Gen 42-44	55	Num 26-28	95	1 Sa 14
16	Gen 45-46	56	Num 29-30	96	1 Sa 15-16
17	Gen 47-49	57	Num 31-32	97	1 Sa 17-19
18	Gen 50; Ex 1-3	58	Num 33-35	98	1 Sa 20-21
19	Ex 4-6	59	Num 36; Deut 1	99	1 Sa 22-24
20	Ex 7-8	60	Deut 2-3	100	1 Sa 25-26
21	Ex 9-11	61	Deut 4-6	101	1 Sa 27-30
22	Ex 12-13	62	Deut 7-9	102	1 Sa 31; 2 Sa 1-2
23	Ex 14-16	63	Deut 10-11	103	2 Sa 3-5
24	Ex 17-20	64	Deut 12-14	104	2 Sa 6-8
25	Ex 21-22	65	Deut 15-17	105	2 Sa 9-11
26	Ex 23-25	66	Deut 18-20	106	2 Sa 12-13
27	Ex 26-28	67	Deut 21-23	107	2 Sa 14-15
28	Ex 29	68	Deut 24-26	108	2 Sa 16-18
29	Ex 30-32	69	Deut 27-28	109	2 Sa 19
30	Ex 33-35	70	Deut 29-30	110	2 Sa 20-22
31	Ex 36-38	71	Deut 31-32	111	2 Sa 23-24
32	Ex 39-40	72	Deut 33-34; Josh 1-2	112	1 Kgs 1-2
33	Lev 1-4	73	Josh 3-5	113	1 Kgs 3-4
34	Lev 5-6	74	Josh 6-7	114	1 Kgs 5-7
35	Lev 7-9	75	Josh 8-10	115	1 Kgs 8
36	Lev 10-12	76	Josh 11-12	116	1 Kgs 9-10
37	Lev 13	77	Josh 13-16	117	1 Kgs 11-12
38	Lev 14-15	78	Josh 17-19	118	1 Kgs 13-14
39	Lev 16-17	79	Josh 20-22	119	1 Kgs 15-16
40	Lev 18-20	80	Josh 23-24	120	1 Kgs 17-18

COVER TO COVER READING PLAN (CONT.)

Day	Reading	Day	Reading	Day	Reading
121	1 Kgs 19-20	161	Neh 7-9	201	Pro 29-31; Ecc 1
122	1 Kgs 21-22	162	Neh 10-11	202	Ecc 2-6
123	2 Kgs 1-3	163	Neh 12-13	203	Ecc 7-10
124	2 Kgs 4	164	Est 1-4	204	Ecc 11-12; Sos 1-4
125	2 Kgs 5-7	165	Est 5-8	205	Sos 5-8; Isa 1
126	2 Kgs 8-9	166	Est 9-10; Job 1-2	206	Isa 2-5
127	2 Kgs 10-11	167	Job 3-8	207	Isa 6-9
128	2 Kgs 12-14	168	Job 9-13	208	Isa 10-13
129	2 Kgs 15-16	169	Job 14-18	209	Isa 14-18
130	2 Kgs 17-18	170	Job 19-23	210	Isa 19-23
131	2 Kgs 19-20	171	Job 24-29	211	Isa 24-27
132	2 Kgs 21-23	172	Job 30-33	212	Isa 28-30
133	2 Kgs 24-25	173	Job 34-38	213	Isa 31-34
134	1 Chr 1-3	174	Job 39-42; Ps 1	214	Isa 35-37
135	1 Chr 4-6	175	Ps 2-10	215	Isa 38-41
136	1 Chr 7-8	176	Ps 11-18	216	Isa 42-44
137	1 Chr 9-11	177	Ps 19-26	217	Isa 45-48
138	1 Chr 12-15	178	Ps 27-34	218	Isa 49-51
139	1 Chr 16-18	179	Ps 35-39	219	Isa 52-56
140	1 Chr 19-22	180	Ps 40-47	220	Isa 57-60
141	1 Chr 23-25	181	Ps 48-55	221	Isa 61-64
142	1 Chr 26-28	182	Ps 56-63	222	Isa 65-66; Jer 1
143	1 Chr 29; 2 Chr 1-2	183	Ps 64-69	223	Jer 2-4
144	2 Chr 3-5	184	Ps 70-76	224	Jer 5-6
145	2 Chr 6-8	185	Ps 77-80	225	Jer 7-9
146	2 Chr 9-12	186	Ps 81-88	226	Jer 10-12
147	2 Chr 13-16	187	Ps 89-96	227	Jer 13-15
148	2 Chr 17-19	188	Ps 97-104	228	Jer 16-18
149	2 Chr 20-22	189	Ps 105-107	229	Jer 19-22
150	2 Chr 23-25	190	Ps 108-117	230	Jer 23-24
151	2 Chr 26-28	191	Ps 118-119	231	Jer 25-27
152	2 Chr 29-30	192	Ps 120-133	232	Jer 28-29
153	2 Chr 31-32	193	Ps 134-142	233	Jer 30-31
154	2 Chr 33-35	194	Ps 143-150; Pro 1	234	Jer 32-33
155	2 Chr 36; Ezr 1-2	195	Pro 2-6	235	Jer 34-36
156	Ezr 3-5	196	Pro 7-11	236	Jer 37-39
157	Ezr 6-7	197	Pro 12-15	237	Jer 40-42
158	Ezr 8-10	198	Pro 16-19	238	Jer 43-45
159	Neh 1-3	199	Pro 20-24	239	Jer 46-48
160	Neh 4-6	200	Pro 25-28	240	Jer 49-50

COVER TO COVER READING PLAN (CONT.)

Day	Reading	Day	Reading	Day	Reading
241	Jer 51	283	Mat 5-7	325	Acts 12-13
242	Jer 52; Lam 1	284	Mat 8-9	326	Acts 14-16
243	Lam 2-4	285	Mat 10-12	327	Acts 17-19
244	Lam 5; Eze 1-3	286	Mat 13-14	328	Acts 20-21
245	Eze 4-6	287	Mat 15-17	329	Acts 22-23
246	Eze 7-10	288	Mat 18-20	330	Acts 24-26
247	Eze 11-13	289	Mat 21-22	331	Acts 27-28; Rom 1
248	Eze 14-16	290	Mat 23-24	332	Rom 2-4
249	Eze 17-18	291	Mat 25-26	333	Rom 5-8
250	Eze 19-20	292	Mat 27-28	334	Rom 9-11
251	Eze 21-22	293	Mk 1-3	335	Rom 12-15
252	Eze 23-24	294	Mk 4-5	336	Rom 16; 1 Co 1-3
253	Eze 25-27	295	Mk 6-8	337	1 Co 4-7
254	Eze 28-30	296	Mk 9-10	338	1 Co 8-11
255	Eze 31-32	297	Mk 11-12	339	1 Co 12-14
256	Eze 33-35	298	Mk 13-14	340	1 Co 15-16; 2 Co 1
257	Eze 36-37	299	Mk 15-16	341	2 Co 2-6
258	Eze 38-39	300	Luk 1-2	342	2 Co 7-10
259	Eze 40-42	301	Luk 3-4	343	2 Co 11-13; Gal 1-2
260	Eze 43-44	302	Luk 5-6	344	Gal 3-5
261	Eze 45-46	303	Luk 7-8	345	Gal 6; Eph 1-4
262	Eze 47-48; Dan 1	304	Luk 9	346	Eph 5-6; Phil 1
263	Dan 2-3	305	Luk 10-11	347	Phil 2-4; Col 1
264	Dan 4-5	306	Luk 12-13	348	Col 2-4; 1 Th 1-2
265	Dan 6-7	307	Luk 14-16	349	1 Th 3-5; 2 Th 1-3
266	Dan 8-9	308	Luk 17-19	350	1 Ti 1-6
267	Dan 10-11	309	Luk 20-21	351	2 Ti 1-4; Tit 1
268	Dan 12; Hos 1-4	310	Luk 22-23	352	Tit 2-3; Phlm; Heb 1-3
269	Hos 5-10	311	Luk 24; John 1	353	Heb 4-8
270	Hos 11-14; Joe 1	312	John 2-4	354	Heb 9-10
271	Joe 2-3; Amo 1-2	313	John 5-6	355	Heb 11-13; Jam 1
272	Amo 3-7	314	John 7	356	Jam 2-5
273	Amo 8-9; Oba; Jon 1	315	John 8-9	357	1 Pe 1-5
274	Jon 2-4; Mic 1-3	316	John 10-11	358	2 Pe 1-3; 1 Jn 1
275	Mic 4-7; Nah 1	317	John 12-14	359	1 Jn 2-5
276	Nah 2-3; Hab 1-3	318	John 15-17	360	2 Jn; 3 Jn; Jude; Rev 1-2
277	Zep 1-3; Hag 1	319	John 18-19	361	Rev 3-6
278	Hag 2; Zec 1-4	320	John 20-21; Acts 1	362	Rev 7-10
279	Zec 5-9	321	Acts 2-4	363	Rev 11-15
280	Zec 10-14	322	Acts 5-7	364	Rev 16-18
281	Mal 1-4	323	Acts 8-9	365	Rev 19-22
282	Mat 1-4	324	Acts 10-11		

CHRONOLOGICAL READING PLAN

This reading plan will also have you read the Bible in a year; however, the daily reading is organized in chronological order from when they occur in history. For example, Job takes place after Genesis 11 but before Genesis 12. This is one of my favorite reading plans and one that has helped me better understand the Bible.

Day	Reading	Day	Reading	Day	Reading
1	Gen 1-3	41	Ex 33-35	81	Deut 32-34, Ps 91
2	Gen 4-7	42	Ex 36-38	82	Josh 1-4
3	Gen 8-11	43	Ex 39-40	83	Josh 5-8
4	Job 1-5	44	Lev 1-4	84	Josh 9-11
5	Job 6-9	45	Lev 5-7	85	Josh 12-15
6	Job 10-13	46	Lev 8-10	86	Josh 16-18
7	Job 14-16	47	Lev 11-13	87	Josh 19-21
8	Job 17-20	48	Lev 14-15	88	Josh 22-24
9	Job 21-23	49	Lev 16-18	89	Judg 1-2
10	Job 24-28	50	Lev 19-21	90	Judg 3-5
11	Job 29-31	51	Lev 22-23	91	Judg 6-7
12	Job 32-34	52	Lev 24-25	92	Judg 8-9
13	Job 35-37	53	Lev 26-27	93	Judg 10-12
14	Job 38-39	54	Num 1-2	94	Judg 13-15
15	Job 40-42	55	Num 3-4	95	Judg 16-18
16	Gen 12-15	56	Num 5-6	96	Judg 19-21
17	Gen 16-18	57	Num 7	97	Ruth 1-4
18	Gen 19-21	58	Num 8-10	98	1 Sam 1-3
19	Gen 22-24	59	Num 11-13	99	1 Sam 4-8
20	Gen 25-26	60	Num 14-15, Ps 90	100	1 Sam 9-12
21	Gen 27-29	61	Num 16-17	101	1 Sam 13-14
22	Gen 30-31	62	Num 18-20	102	1 Sam 15-17
23	Gen 32-34	63	Num 21-22	103	1 Sam 18-20, Ps 11, Ps 59
24	Gen 35-37	64	Num 23-25	104	1 Sam 21-24
25	Gen 38-40	65	Num 26-27	105	Ps 7, Ps 27, Ps 31, Ps 34, Ps 52
26	Gen 41-42	66	Num 28-30	106	Ps 56, Ps 120, Ps 140-142
27	Gen 43-45	67	Num 31-32	107	1 Sam 25-27
28	Gen 46-47	68	Num 33-34	108	Ps 17, Ps 35, Ps 54, Ps 63
29	Gen 48-50	69	Num 35-36	109	1 Sam 28-31, Ps 18
30	Ex 1-3	70	Deut 1-2	110	Ps 121, Ps 123-125, Ps 128-130
31	Ex 4-6	71	Deut 3-4	111	2 Sam 1-4
32	Ex 7-9	72	Deut 5-7	112	Ps 6, Ps 8-10, Ps 14, Ps 16, Ps 19, Ps 21
33	Ex 10-12	73	Deut 8-10	113	1 Chr 1-2
34	Ex 13-15	74	Deut 11-13	114	Ps 43-45, Ps 49, Ps 84-85, Ps 87
35	Ex 16-18	75	Deut 14-16	115	1 Chr 3-5
36	Ex 19-21	76	Deut 17-20	116	Ps 73, Ps 77-78
37	Ex 22-24	77	Deut 21-23	117	1 Chr 6
38	Ex 25-27	78	Deut 24-27	118	Ps 81, Ps 88, Ps 92-93
39	Ex 28-29	79	Deut 28-29	119	1 Chr 7-10
40	Ex 30-32	80	Deut 30-31	120	Ps 102-104

CHRONOLOGICAL READING PLAN (CONT.)

Day	Reading	Day	Reading	Day	Reading
121	2 Sam 5:1-10, 1 Chr 11-12	161	Prov 22-24	201	Hos 1-7
122	Ps 133	162	1 Kgs 5-6, 2 Chr 2-3	202	Hos 8-14
123	Ps 106-107	163	1 Kgs 7, 2 Chr 4	203	Isa 28-30
124	2 Sam 5:11-6:23, 1 Chr 13-16	164	1 Kgs 8, 2 Chr 5	204	Isa 31-34
125	Ps 1-2, Ps 15, Ps 22-24, Ps 47, Ps 68	165	2 Chr 6-7, Ps 136	205	Isa 35-36
126	Ps 89, Ps 96, Ps 100, Ps 101, Ps 105, Ps 132	166	Ps 134, Ps 146-150	206	Isa 37-39, Ps 76
127	2 Sam 7, 1 Chr 17	167	1 Kgs 9, 2 Chr 8	207	Isa 40-43
128	Ps 25, Ps 29, Ps 33, Ps 36, Ps 39	168	Prov 25-26	208	Isa 44-48
129	2 Sam 8-9, 1 Chr 18	169	Prov 27-29	209	2 Kgs 18:9-19:37, Ps 46, Ps 80, Ps 135
130	Ps 50, Ps 53, Ps 60, Ps 75	170	Eccl 1-6	210	Isa 49-53
131	2 Sam 10, 1 Chr 19, Ps 20	171	Eccl 7-12	211	Isa 54-58
132	Ps 65-67, Ps 69-70	172	1 Kgs 10-11, 2 Chr 9	212	Isa 59-63
133	2 Sam 11-12, 1 Chr 20	173	Prov 30-31	213	Isa 64-66
134	Ps 32, Ps 51, Ps 86, Ps 122	174	1 Kgs 12-14	214	2 Kgs 20-21
135	2 Sam 13-15	175	2 Chr 10-12	215	2 Chr 32-33
136	Ps 3-4, Ps 12-13, Ps 28, Ps 55	176	1 Kgs 15:1-24, 2 Chr 13-16	216	Nahum 1-3
137	2 Sam 16-18	177	1 Kgs 15:25-16:34, 2 Chr 17	217	2 Kgs 22-23, 2 Chr 34-35
138	Ps 26, Ps 40, Ps 58, Ps 61-62, Ps 64	178	1 Kgs 17-19	218	Zeph 1-3
139	2 Sam 19-21	179	1 Kgs 20-21	219	Jer 1-3
140	Ps 5, Ps 38, Ps 41-42	180	1 Kgs 22, 2 Chr 18	220	Jer 4-6
141	2 Sam 22-23, Ps 57	181	2 Chr 19-23	221	Jer 7-9
142	Ps 95, Ps 97-99	182	Obad 1, Ps 82-83	222	Jer 10-13
143	2 Sam 24, 1 Chr 21-22, Ps 30	183	2 Kgs 1-4	223	Jer 14-17
144	Ps 108-110	184	2 Kgs 5-8	224	Jer 18-22
145	1 Chr 23-25	185	2 Kgs 9-11	225	Jer 23-25
146	Ps 131, Ps 138-139, Ps 143-145	186	2 Kgs 12-13, 2 Chr 24	226	Jer 26-29
147	1 Chr 26-29, Ps 127	187	2 Kgs 14, 2 Chr 25	227	Jer 30-31
148	Ps 111-118	188	Jonah 1-4	228	Jer 32-34
149	1 Kgs 1-2, Ps 37, Ps 71, Ps 94	189	2 Kgs 15, 2 Chr 26	229	Jer 35-37
150	Ps 119:1-88	190	Isa 1-4	230	Jer 38-40, Ps 74, Ps 79
151	1 Kgs 3-4, 2 Chr 1, Ps 72	191	Isa 5-8	231	2 Kgs 24-25, 2 Chr 36
152	Ps 119:89-176	192	Amos 1-5	232	Hab 1-3
153	Sng 1-8	193	Amos 6-9	233	Jer 41-45
154	Prov 1-3	194	2 Chr 27, Isa 9-12	234	Jer 46-48
155	Prov 4-6	195	Mic 1-7	235	Jer 49-50
156	Prov 7-9	196	2 Chr 28, 2 Kgs 16-17	236	Jer 51-52
157	Prov 10-12	197	Isa 13-17	237	Lam 1:1-3:36
158	Prov 13-15	198	Isa 18-22	238	Lam 3:37-5:22
159	Prov 16-18	199	Isa 23-27	239	Ezek 1-4
160	Prov 19-21	200	2 Kgs 18:1-8, 2 Chr 29-31, Ps 48	240	Ezek 5-8

CHRONOLOGICAL READING PLAN (CONT.)

Day	Reading
241	Ezek 9-12
242	Ezek 13-15
243	Ezek 16-17
244	Ezek 18-19
245	Ezek 20-21
246	Ezek 22-23
247	Ezek 24-27
248	Ezek 28-31
249	Ezek 32-34
250	Ezek 35-37
251	Ezek 38-39
252	Ezek 40-41
253	Ezek 42-43
254	Ezek 44-45
255	Ezek 46-48
256	Joel 1-3
257	Dan 1-3
258	Dan 4-6
259	Dan 7-9
260	Dan 10-12
261	Ezra 1-3
262	Ezra 4-6, Ps 137
263	Hag 1-2
264	Zech 1-7
265	Zech 8-14
266	Est 1-5
267	Est 6-10
268	Ezra 7-10
269	Neh 1-5
270	Neh 6-7
271	Neh 8-10
272	Neh 11-13, Ps 126
273	Mal 1-4
274	Luke 1, John 1:1-14
275	Matt 1, Luke 2:1-38
276	Matt 2, Luke 2:39-52
277	Matt 3, Mark 1, Luke 3
278	Matt 4, Luke 4-5, John 1:15-51
279	John 2-4
280	Mark 2
281	John 5
282	Matt 12:1-21, Mark 3, Luke 6

Day	Reading
283	Matt 5-7
284	Matt 8:1-13, Luke 7
285	Matt 11
286	Matt 12:22-50, Luke 11
287	Matt 13, Luke 8
288	Matt 8:14-34, Mark 4-5
289	Matt 9-10
290	Matt 14, Mark 6, Luke 9:1-17
291	John 6
292	Matt 15, Mark 7
293	Matt 16, Mark 8, Luke 9:18-27
294	Matt 17, Mark 9, Luke 9:28-62
295	Matt 18
296	John 7-8
297	John 9:1-10:21
298	Luke 10-11, John 10:22-42
299	Luke 12-13
300	Luke 14-15
301	Luke 16-17:10
302	John 11
303	Luke 17:11-18:14
304	Matt 19, Mark 10
305	Matt 20-21
306	Luke 18:15-19:48
307	Mark 11, John 12
308	Matt 22, Mark 12
309	Matt 23, Luke 20-21
310	Mark 13
311	Matt 24
312	Matt 25
313	Matt 26, Mark 14
314	Luke 22, John 13
315	John 14-17
316	Matt 27, Mark 15
317	Luke 23, John 18-19
318	Matt 28, Mark 16
319	Luke 24, John 20-21
320	Acts 1-3
321	Acts 4-6
322	Acts 7-8
323	Acts 9-10
324	Acts 11-12

Day	Reading
325	Acts 13-14
326	Jas 1-5
327	Acts 15-16
328	Gal 1-3
329	Gal 4-6
330	Acts 17-18:18
331	1 Thes 1-5, 2 Thes 1-3
332	Acts 18:19-19:41
333	1 Cor 1-4
334	1 Cor 5-8
335	1 Cor 9-11
336	1 Cor 12-14
337	1 Cor 15-16
338	2 Cor 1-4
339	2 Cor 5-9
340	2 Cor 10-13
341	Acts 20:1-3, Rom 1-3
342	Rom 4-7
343	Rom 8-10
344	Rom 11-13
345	Rom 14-16
346	Acts 20:4-23:35
347	Acts 24-26
348	Acts 27-28
349	Col 1-4, Phm 1
350	Eph 1-6
351	Phil 1-4
352	1 Tim 1-6
353	Titus 1-3
354	1 Pet 1-5
355	Heb 1-6
356	Heb 7-10
357	Heb 11-13
358	2 Tim 1-4
359	2 Pet 1-3, Jude 1
360	1 Jn 1-5
361	2 Jn 1, 3 Jn 1
362	Rev 1-5
363	Rev 6-11
364	Rev 12-18
365	Rev 19-22

Appendix C
Glossary

Most of the definitions provided in this book are quoted from Wayne Grudem's *Systematic Theology*. I highly recommend this book to all Disciples of Christ, especially those who want a deeper understanding of theology. I have found this book to be quite readable and has largely impacted my own spiritual growth. Wayne Grudem is a "Research Professor of Theology and Biblical Studies at Phoenix Seminary in Phoenix, Arizona. He received a B.A. from Harvard University, an M.Div. and a D.D. from Westminster Seminary, Philadelphia, and a Ph.D. (in New Testament) from the University of Cambridge, England."[1]

Atonement: Reconciliation. "The work Christ did in His life and death to earn our salvation" (Grudem, *Systematic Theology*, 705).

Catechism: A method of teaching using a series of questions and answers.

Christ: Anointed One. Messiah is the Hebrew word for "Anointed One."

Common Grace: "The grace of God by which He gives people innumerable blessings that are not part of salvation" (Grudem, *Systematic Theology*, 803).

Conversion: "Our willing response to the gospel call, in which we sincerely repent of sins and place our trust in Christ for salvation" (Grudem, *Systematic Theology*, 861).

---

[1] "Biography." Wayne Grudem. Accessed December 30, 2020. http://www.waynegrudem.com/about.

Disciple: Learner. Student.

Glorification: "The final step in the application of redemption. It will happen when Christ returns, raises from the dead the bodies of all believers for all time who have died, and reunites them with their souls, and changes the bodies of all believers who remain alive, thereby giving all believers at the same time perfect resurrection bodies like His own" (Grudem, *Systematic Theology*, 1018).

Gospel: Jesus came and died for the sins of mankind so that we may enjoy a genuine relationship with God. Then Jesus was resurrected on the third day of His death, proving that He was who He claimed to be and that He accomplished what He set out to accomplish.

Grace: Undeserved and unearned love. "God's goodness toward those who deserve only punishment" (Grudem, *Systematic Theology*, 239).

Hypostatic Union: "The union of Christ's human and divine natures in one person" (Grudem, *Systematic Theology*, 695).

Incarnation: To become flesh. "The act of God the Son whereby he took to himself a human nature" (Grudem, *Systematic Theology*, 678).

Justification: "An instantaneous legal act of God in which he (1) thinks of our sins as forgiven and Christ's righteousness as belonging to us, and (2) declares us to be righteous in his sight" (Grudem, *Systematic Theology*, 885).

Repentance: Turning from sin and to turn to God. "A heartfelt sorrow for sin, a renouncing of it, and a sincere commitment to forsake it and walk in obedience to Christ" (Grudem, *Systematic Theology*, 865).

Sanctification: "A progressive work of God and believers that makes us more and more free from sin and like Christ in our actual lives" (Grudem, *Systematic Theology*, 924).

Sin: Miss the mark; fall short of God's glory. To rebel against God. "Any failure to conform to the moral law of God in act, attitude, or nature" (Grudem, *Systematic Theology*, 619).

Sin of Commission: Committing an action that God has told us not to do.

Sin of Omission: Omitting to do an action that God has commanded us to do.

Supplication: A request, asking for something.

Trinity: "God eternally exists as three persons, Father, Son, and Holy Spirit, and each person is fully God, and there is one God" (Grudem, *Systematic Theology*, 269).

Appendix D
Scripture Index

* Reference is quoted in the footnote of the page.

187

Made in the USA
Las Vegas, NV
20 September 2021